REGIONAL ECONOMIC COMMUNITIES AND PEACEBUILDING IN AFRICA: THE EXPERIENCES OF ECOWAS AND IGAD

Victor A.O Adetula
Redie Bereketeab
Olugbemi Jaiyebo

NORDISKA AFRIKAINSTITUTET
UPPSALA 2016

INDEXING TERMS:

Regional organizations
Economic relations
Regional integration
Regional cooperation
Regional security
Post-conflict reconstruction
Peacebuilding
Conflict management
Recommendations
West Africa
Horn of Africa

Regional Economic Communities and Peacebuilding in Africa:
The Experiences of ECOWAS and IGAD
NAI Policy Dialogue No 12

Victor A.O Adetula, Redie Bereketeab and Olugbemi Jaiyebo

ISSN 1654-6709
ISBN 978-91-7106-798-2 pb
ISBN 978-91-7106-799-9 pdf
ISBN 978-91-7106-800-2 epub

Cover photo: U.S. Army Africa photo by Staff Sgt. Donna Davis, CC BY 2.0
Language checking: Richard Langlais, AREL Scientific AB
Layout: Henrik Alfredsson, Nordic Africa Institute

Print on demand: Lightning Source UK Ltd.

The opinions expressed in this volume are those of the authors and
do not necessarily reflect the views of the Nordic Africa Institute.

Contents

Preface and acknowledgements

In pursuit of its mission of building networks with research and policy institutions in Africa, NAI collaborated with the Abuja-based Institute for Peace and Conflict Resolution (IPCR), a leading Nigerian government research and policy centre on peace and conflict resolution, to organise a two-day policy dialogue in September 2016. The Africa Peacebuilding Network (APN) of the Social Science Research Council (SSRC) partnered with the two institutions and supported the initiative with financial grant which is most appreciated. Apart from the financial support, APN sponsored and facilitated the participation of some its grantees to the Abuja Policy Dialogue.

The idea of a Policy Dialogue came out of the need to scale up policy engagement on the role of regional economic communities (RECs) in peacebuilding in Africa. Previous and ongoing research activities at the Nordic Africa Institute (NAI) underscore the importance of interaction and shared learning between researchers and policy makers on the performances of Africa's RECs and peacebuilding in Africa. A two-day Policy Dialogue was held in Abuja (1-2 September 2016). The programme generated and elicited comments, observations and recommendations from over eighty participants from ten countries representing a broad range of interests.

Nigeria's Minister of Mines and Steel Development, Dr. Kayode Fayemi, gave the keynote speech titled, "Two and a Half Decades of ECOWAS' Peace Interventions in West Africa: an Insider-Outsider Perspective". He pointed out the successes of ECOWAS in promoting peace and security in West Africa but cautioned against complacency. He advised ECOWAS to revisit and implement relevant recommendations in the reviews and assessments of its programmes, and seek ways of improving collaboration with civil society. Professor Ibrahim Gambari, former Nigeria's Representative to the United Nations, chaired the programme. He noted that after four decades of its existence, ECOWAS cannot be said to be a community despite its laudable achievements in peace in Liberia and Sierra Leone. Professor Gambari drew attention to the need to ensure a balance between ECOWAS' mandate for regional security and the goal of economic integration. He also advocated for increased engagement with the civil society in the activities and operations of regional integration schemes including their peacebuilding functions and responsibilities.

The Institute is grateful to Dr. Kayode Fayemi and Professor Ibrahim Gambari for their presence at both the Policy Dialogue and other follow up activities. Also, NAI puts on record the support of the Ambassador of Finland in Nigeria, HE Ms. Pirjo Suomela-Chowdhury, and the embassies of other Nordic countries in Nigeria.

Iina Soiri
Director, Nordic Africa Institute

Although primarily set up to promote economic integration, Africa's RECs have increasingly taken up a prominent role in conflict resolution and peace support operations

Executive Summary

Chapter Eight of the United Nations Charter recognizes the option of regional institutions taking appropriate action on matters relating to international peace and security, provided such institutions and/or their activities are consistent with the purpose and principles of the UN. Africa, since the end of the Cold War, has recorded increased involvement of its Regional Economic Communities (RECs) in the peacebuilding process. African countries have responded to the challenges of the post-Cold War international system mostly by collectively promoting sub-regional and continental-wide initiatives in conflict resolution and peacebuilding. Admittedly, the existence of many violent conflicts in Africa, as well as their "domino" effects at the sub-regional level, contributed significantly to the growing desire for collective security systems and conflict management mechanisms. The broadening of the role and functions of African regional organizations to include responsibility for peacebuilding and conflict management generally adds credence to the efficacy of regional integration. Many issues, however, present themselves in the engagement of RECs with the peacebuilding process in Africa. The Nordic Africa Institute (NAI), Uppsala, in collaboration with the Abuja-based Institute for Peace and Conflict Resolution (IPCR), and in partnership with the Social Science Research Council-Africa Peacebuilding Network (APN-SS-RC), had a policy dialogue on the need to scale up policy engagement on the role of RECs in peacebuilding in Africa. Previous and ongoing research activities at the NAI underscore the importance of interaction and shared learning between researchers and policymakers on the performance of Africa's RECs in peacebuilding.

The performance of Africa's regional organizations in ensuring peace and security on the continent through its peacebuilding activities was the focus of the Policy Dialogue. Although primarily set up to promote economic integration, Africa's RECs have increasingly taken up a prominent role in conflict resolution and peace support operations, as evident in the recent peace processes in Burundi, Liberia, Sierra Leone, Guinea, Guinea-Bissau, Mali, Cote d'Ivoire, Zimbabwe, Mali, Congo DRC, Sudan, and South Sudan, among others. The intervention of the Economic Community of West African States (ECOWAS) in the Liberian crisis was the first experiment by a sub-regional organization in post-Cold War Africa. The lessons learned from peacekeeping and mediation efforts in Liberia and Sierra Leone in the early years of the ECOWAS/ ECOWAS Cease-Fire Operation Monitoring Operation Group (ECOMOG) contributed to the consolidation of mechanisms for conflict prevention and peacebuilding in West Africa.

More recently, other regional economic communities on the continent have replicated the example of the ECOWAS 'success story' in peace mediation, peacebuilding and peacekeeping. For example, the Intergovernmental Authority on Development (IGAD) has played important roles in the resolution of conflicts in the Horn of Africa. IGAD had initially been set up to address natural resource management and development in the Horn of Africa, before taking on board conflict management, peace and security roles on a regional basis. The records of IGAD and ECOWAS with regard to promoting peace, stability and development in their respective regions are mixed. In spite of the challenges they face, RECs are capable of playing important roles with regard to peace mediation, peacekeeping and peacebuilding. This calls for a comparative perspective on the roles of the ECOWAS and IGAD, in relation to regional peace and security in the West, as well as the Horn of Africa, and the exploration of new ideas and actions that are likely to strengthen their capacity to effectively address the peace-building challenges facing both regions. A closer look at the conflict management and peacebuilding activities of ECOWAS and IGAD reveals the following:

i.   the growing complexity of conflict dynamics and security challenges in the post-Cold War world require greater cooperation and coordination among states within regions. In this regard, enhanced status and roles for regional organizations in conflict management, peacekeeping and peacebuilding are important features of the emerging post-Cold War system;

ii.   the intrinsic linkages between peacebuilding and development underscore the importance of the social and economic dimensions that are heightening and sustaining the conflict dynamics in Africa. Although the Economic Community of West African States (ECOWAS) and the Intergovernmental Authority on Development (IGAD) were originally established to promote economic integration, their mandates have been expanded to include broad peacebuilding and regional security functions;

iii. ECOWAS and IGAD have been involved in peacebuilding, recording varying levels of success and failure. Current peacebuilding initiatives by ECOWAS and IGAD have emphasized a military approach over soft approaches to peacebuilding. The involvement of member states of ECOWAS and IGAD in peacebuilding interventions has been a high cost and risk for national economies and regional economic integration programmes;

iv.   the influence, power and geostrategic interests of the pivotal states in both ECOWAS and IGAD have implications for peacebuilding interventions in their respective regions. Also, the challenges of internal insecurity and economic recession that confront member-states of ECOWAS and IGAD have largely impeded their performance in ensuring regional peace and stability within their respective regions. Member states of ECOWAS and IGAD are still challenged by the structural crisis of statehood, and are threatened by poor economies, youth bulge and incidences of youth unemployment and underemployment;

v.   research and documentation of the experiences of African RECs in peacebuilding have not received adequate attention, which in turn has implications, for lessons learned, and benefits, for future planning, policy formulation and implementation.

Key Recommendations:

i.   there is a need for the Economic Community of West African States (ECOWAS) and the Intergovernmental Authority on Development (IGAD) to periodically review their guiding principles, to address new realities and challenges at global and regional levels, in order to effectively promote economic integration and, as well, address the structural crisis of statehood and other underlying causes of violent conflict in their respective regions;

ii. ECOWAS and IGAD should develop legal and institutional frameworks for inclusive partnerships, and network for sustainable peacebuilding interventions in their respective regions;

iii. peacebuilding initiatives by ECOWAS and IGAD should include deliberate policies and programmes that address the problems of youth unemployment and underemployment;

iv. ECOWAS and IGAD should work towards effective harmonization of their mandates and programmes on regional economic integration and peacebuilding for sustainable development;

v.   member states of ECOWAS and IGAD should demonstrate more commitment to the development of RECs, as well as active involvement in ensuring regional peace and security, through prompt attention to their financial obligations and compliance with treaty provisions, protocols and resolutions;

vi. ECOWAS and IGAD should insist on the application of broad and integrative approaches to peacebuilding before, during, and after conflicts;

vii. ECOWAS and IGAD should accord greater importance to research and documentation and acknowledge the link between research and policy formulation and implementation;

viii. ECOWAS and IGAD should enhance incorporation of early warning signals in their peacebuilding programmes;

ix. ECOWAS and IGAD should reinvigorate efforts towards effective partnership with credible civil society organizations in the areas of peacebuilding and development;

x.   ECOWAS and IGAD should ensure adequate gender mainstreaming in all their peacebuilding programmes and activities;

xi. ECOWAS and IGAD should advocate the establishment and development of multinational taskforces in their respective regions, to help combat international terrorism and other cross-border crimes;

xii. financial self-sufficiency of RECs cannot be overemphasized, because it is critical to the sustainability and local ownership of peace support operations by ECOWAS and IGAD.

The present neo-liberal world order under United States hegemony makes a "regionalist" approach a compelling option for many states in the Global South

1. Introduction

The complexity of security challenges in the post-bipolar world requires greater coopera-tion and coordination among states within a region. Also, the present neo-liberal world order under United States hegemony makes a "regionalist" approach a compelling option for many states in the Global South, in a world system that is increasingly hierarchically structured. It is within this context that regions of the world are now being reorganized into effective and efficient units of the neo-liberal world system. The US-sponsored African Growth and Opportunity Act (AGOA) and the Economic Partnership Agreement (EPAs) between the European Union and the African, Caribbean and Pacific Group of States (ACP Group) best illustrate this trend. With respect to the maintenance of global peace, the United Nations Security Council (UNSC) is supporting the devolution of some securi-ty responsibilities to regional organizations. In effect, states are expected to submit disputes to regional organizations. In the case of the African continent, the RECs are subsumed within the African Union (AU) organizational structures as component units, and are given functions and responsibilities as representatives of AU at the regional level. In other words, regional matters have to pass through the RECs as component units of AU "en route" to the global system represented by the United Nations. In this global hierarchical structure, African RECs are expected to perform functions and responsibilities that have far-reaching consequences for global peace and security. The inability of many national governments to effectively address problems that have cross-border dimensions has further facilitated the "regionalist approach." In the areas of both economic development and security, many states are now in favour of using regional organisations and other forms of alliances.

The participation of regional organizations in the establishment and maintenance of peace and security is not a recent development. Chapter VIII of the Charter of the Uni-ted Nations contains relevant provisions on roles for "regional arrangements or agencies dealing with such matters relating to the maintenance of international peace and securi-ty." Such regional arrangements and agencies are to compliment the UNSC, which has the primary responsibility for the maintenance of international peace and security, and "no enforcement action shall be taken under regional arrangements or by regional agen-cies without the authorization of the Security Council, with the exception of measures against an enemy state." In addition, regional arrangements and agencies are expected to have adequate capacity to undertake such action, which of course should be "either on the initiative of the states concerned or by reference from the Security Council." Deve-lopments since the end of the Cold War present several opportunities that "increased the chances of finding regional solutions" (Wallensteen, 2012, 4). In Europe, Germany and the United Kingdom became serious about the promotion of regional security in Europe by using regional organizations and other forms of alliances. In Asia, Japan and China have taken up the responsibilities of regional actors. In Africa, the regional approach to development, conflict prevention and management, as the promotion of good governan-ce, is becoming popular among state and non-state actors alike (Adetula, 2015a).

The management of international violence since the end of the Cold War has imposed more responsibilities on regional organizations in Africa. Consequently, the motives for economic cooperation and integration in the region have been broadened to include political interests and regional collective security in addition to the need for greater international bargaining power. The intervention of the Economic Community of West African States (ECOWAS) in the Liberian crisis was the first experiment with intervention by a sub-regional organization in post-Cold War Africa. It is interesting to know that the lessons learned from peacekeeping and mediation efforts in Liberia and Sierra Leone, in the early years of ECOWAS/ECOMOG, contributed to the consolidation of mechanisms for conflict prevention and peacebuilding in West Africa. More recently, other RECs on the continent have replicated the example of the ECOWAS "success story" in peace mediation, peacebuilding, and peacekeeping. For example, the Intergovernmental Authority on Development (IGAD), which was initially set up to address natural resource management and development, has played important roles in the resolution of conflicts in the Horn of Africa. The records of the IGAD and ECOWAS in promoting peace, stability, and development in their respective regions are, however, mixed. Notwithstanding the challenges they face, African RECs have demonstrated the potential for playing important roles in peace mediation, peacekeeping, and peacebuilding. However, several issues present themselves in peacebuilding activities and other related REC interventions. For example, having the realm of domestic affairs of the affected countries unilaterally controlled by external actors can pose some difficulties. Dealing with these requires that definite legal frameworks and clear normative standards guide the peacebuilding process. Existing African RECs were generally set up primarily to promote economic integration. Therefore, their original mandates were tilted towards economic goals and objectives and with less attention to their new roles in peacebuilding (Jaiyebo & Adetula, 2016).

The challenges and realities of the post-Cold War international system have further raised the stakes for the African RECs. The international system presently rests on a fragmented global governance architecture. The multilateral system is not working at its best, in spite of the rhetoric of states about their commitment in support of global cooperative responses. With the end of the Cold War, the powerful and rich countries in the global North have redefined their national interests, which they have reorganized in less altruistic ways (Adetula, 2015). The global North seems not quite interested in assisting Africa and other vulnerable regions in overcoming the constraining effects of global pressures. While this goes on, the world is being treated to the emergence of new global powers, notably Brazil, Russia, India, and China (BRIC). The BRIC states are increasingly involved in current global issues such as global trade, international security, and climate change and energy politics. However, while they have shown global interests, they are not themselves necessarily prepared to assume responsibility for international development, including global peace and security. These developments provided opportunities for regional actors such as the RECs to become more engaged in responsibilities for conflict management and maintenance of regional security. This of course requires deep consideration for seeing peacebuilding as a development process.

2. Peacebuilding as development practice

Peacebuilding refers to a full range of initiatives, strategies, and activities that prevent, reduce, and transform conflicts and develop institutions, attitudes, and relationships that promote sustainable peace and development (Lederach & Appleby, 2010). In this way, peacebuilding activities aim not only to end violence, but to create structures that contribute to a just and sustainable peace (Lederach, 2003). Peacebuilding covers a wide range of policy and intervention areas, from security, reconciliation and justice, and building socio-economic foundations, to constructing a political framework for the society. These intervention areas have evolved over the years and are now understood by some as a "peacebuilding palette" (Killick & Srikantha, 2005). Peacebuilding practice entails the organization and coordination of resources and approaches to achieve multiple goals and address multiple issues on a long-term basis (Schirch, 2004). While it is possible to claim that various aspects of peacebuilding have been experienced at different times in history, peacebuilding as a theoretical construct and development practice has assumed prominence only recently.

Arguably, the end of the Cold War introduced some changes in the principles and practice of conflict management. The growing prominence of "peacebuilding" since the end of the Cold War is not unrelated to the global currents that are associated with the "new" neoliberal world order. Thus, as part of the Western hegemonic agenda, peacebuilding promotes neoliberal values as universal norms. Within this context, an aggressive interventionist approach is imposed on peacebuilding practice. Also, peacebuilding interventions offer excellent opportunities for converting post-conflict societies and other societies under stress into "modern" societies guided by Western values. The source of their stress is wrongly diagnosed as a lack of a sufficient dose of neoliberal values and norms, while the main remedy for the dysfunctionality of fragile societies is regime change, in order to create a conducive environment for the inauguration of neoliberal policies and programmes. The direct contrast to the neoliberal approach to peacebuilding is the "popular progressive" peacebuilding model, which builds on the culture, history, social, and political structures and forces of conflict and post/conflict societies. Popular progressive peacebuilding is historical, contemporary, and at the same time futuristic. It represents a process of continuity, evolution, and metamorphosis in time and space. It also represents space where historical-legal, socio-economic, and politico-cultural idiosyncrasies and edifices play decisive roles (Bereketeab, 2016). In this way, peacebuilding is profoundly concerned with the project of society construction, including nation and state formation through an evolutionary and gradualist process. Some elements of the neoliberal peacebuilding model can be adapted to form a subset of the progressive peacebuilding system, especially in the short term. However, in the long term, peacebuilding pertains to gradual evolutionary pacification of society and emancipation of the state.

Africa, with almost the highest record of violent conflicts in the world, the regional peacekeeping approach must necessarily go beyond the debate of nomenclature to include creative planning, designing, and implementation of peacebuilding interventions that envisage the entire spectrum of short-term emergency, medium-term transition, and long-term development phases. Thus, peacebuilding is better conceived and practiced as an integrated process with elements that include the prevention and resolution of violent conflict; the consolidation of peace, once violence has been reduced through systematically organized mediation and reconciliation; and post-conflict reconstruction, with a view to avoiding lapses that lead to violent conflict. There are different levels in a conflict, and conflict resolution arrangement must consider and align all of them towards the attainment of sustainable peace (Adetula, 2015a, 57). Conceived in this way, interventions by the international community, notably the UN, regional and sub-regional organizations, donors, and development partners should be designed to emphasize commitment to "positive peace," which in addition to the absence of violence seeks for socio-economic security, equity, and participation in post-conflict situations. For instance, interventions and peace operations should target the provision of basic services in conflict zones, while they encourage the civil population to own the peace process. This is the context in which peacebuilding is seen as "development practice" (Adetula, 2015b, 58).

The concept of "peacebuilding" is still evolving in international law. As expected, this has implications for its role and status in how regional actors like the RECs manage conflicts. When it was initially propositioned into the international lexicon, it encapsulated action in identifying and supporting structures that tend to strengthen and solidify peace in order to avoid a relapse into conflict (United Nations, 1992). Thus, within the UN system, peacebuilding has assumed a meaning beyond mere avoidance of conflict, to include the promotion of social justice and equity, along with the associated commitment to eliminating the root causes of conflict, such as poverty and inequality. Although there now seems to be a clear direction in thinking, the precise meaning of peacebuilding as an operational concept has yet to be defined (Hamilton & Wachs, 2008). However, the UN uses the concept of "peacebuilding" to cover several aspects of the peace process. This has been taken to mean, among other things, "reforming or strengthening governmental institutions," or "the creation of structures for the institutionalization of peace" (Chesterman, 2005). Experience to date has shown that "regional peacebuilding constitutes a new challenge to peace practice and research. It is an important notion but has seldom had the focus that is required" (Wallesteen, 2012, 3). Notwithstanding that, the increased attention to regional organization and the growing prominence of regional solutions to the maintenance of global peace makes the regional peacebuilding approach a sine qua non for regional organizations.

The notion that "all Africans are the same" further enhances the regional dimension of conflicts in Africa. The region harbours people of common history, traditions and customs that are separated by national boundaries under the modern state system (Adetula, 2015). The implication for the region is "that neighbouring countries are not only affected by refugee flows, disruption flows, disruption of transportation routes and smuggling of weapons," and complicity of governments of neighbouring countries in conflicts is a regular occurrence (2012, 3). In Africa there are many examples of conflicts that started in one specific area but later engulfed the entire region. The physical and demographic features of Africa and the porosity of its borders make it easy for environment-induced conflicts to assume a regional character. It is in this context, for instance, that climate change, desertification, famine, and drought are considered as threats to regional peace and security in West, East and Central Africa.

Another factor that promotes the regional character of African conflict is the existence of social and economic networks that are built around informal trading, and occupational and religious activities across many states that date back to the pre-colonial period (Adetula, 2003). The historical links among the populations in Africa have been replaced or transformed into contemporary transnational networks. In recent times, new migrant networks, trading networks, and religious movements with complex organizational structures and institutions have emerged in the region. Globalization has significantly changed the character and intensity of armed conflict in Africa. With the benefits of advanced communication technologies, "major engines of globalization" have penetrated national frontiers, creating transnational identities that challenge national solidarity. It is possible to argue that globalization is the primary cause of most of the new wars on the continent (Adetula, 2015b).

SADC
Southern African Development Community

- Angola
- Botswana
- Congo-Kinshasa
- Lesotho
- Madagascar
- Malawi
- Mauritius
- Mozambique
- Namibia
- Seychelles
- South Africa
- Swaziland
- Tanzania
- Zambia
- Zimbabwe

CEN-SAD
Community of Sahel-Saharan States

- Benin
- Burkina Faso
- Central African Republic
- Chad
- Comoros
- Djibouti
- Egypt
- Eritrea
- Gambia
- Ghana
- Guinea
- Guinea-Bissau
- Ivory Coast
- Kenya
- Liberia
- Libya
- Mali
- Morocco
- Niger
- Nigeria
- São Tomé & Príncipe
- Senegal
- Sierra Leone
- Somalia
- Sudan
- Togo
- Tunisia

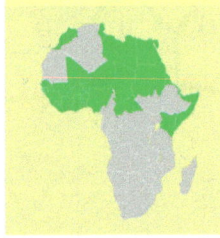

ECCAS
Economic Community of Central African States

- Angola
- Burundi
- Cameroon
- Central African Republic
- Chad
- Congo-Brazzaville
- Congo-Kinshasa
- Equatorial Guinea
- Gabon
- Rwanda
- São Tomé & Príncipe

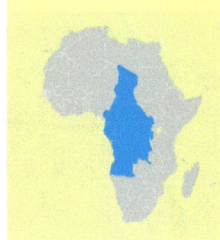

EAC
East African Community

- Burundi
- Kenya
- Rwanda
- South Sudan
- Tanzania
- Uganda

AMU
Arab Maghreb Union

- Algeria
- Libya
- Mauritania
- Morocco
- Tunisia

COMESA
Common Market for Eastern and Southern Africa

- Burundi
- Comoros
- Congo-Kinshasa
- Djibouti
- Eritrea
- Ethiopia
- Egypt
- Kenya
- Libya
- Madagascar
- Malawi
- Mauritius
- Rwanda
- Seychelles
- Sudan
- Swaziland
- Uganda
- Zambia
- Zimbabwe

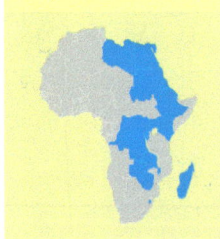

IGAD
Intergovernmental Authority on Development

- Djibouti
- Eritrea
- Ethiopia
- Kenya
- Somalia
- South Sudan
- Sudan
- Uganda

ECOWAS
Economic Community of West African States

- Benin
- Burkina Faso
- Cape Verde
- Gambia
- Ghana
- Guinea
- Guinea-Bissau
- Ivory Coast
- Liberia
- Mali
- Niger
- Nigeria
- Senegal
- Sierra Leone
- Togo

AU
African Union

All states except Morocco

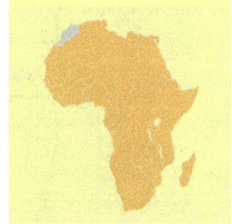

The AU and the RECs. Africa's Regional Economic Communities (RECs) include eight sub-regional bodies which are the building blocks of the African Economic Community established in the 1991 Abuja Treaty which provides the overarching framework for continental economic integration. Africa's RECs do not only constitute key building blocks for economic integration in Africa, but are also key actors working in collaboration with the African Union (AU), in ensuring peace and stability in their regions.

3. Africa's regional economic communities – an overview

The establishment of the Organization of African Unity (OAU), in 1963, represents the consolidation of the gradualist approach to African unity, as well as the broad issue of African development. The role of the Economic Commission of Africa (ECA) in the promotion of regional integration in Africa is well documented in the literature on African development. Many African countries that favoured OAU's gradualist approach to African unity easily became disciples of ECA's gospel of self-reliance and autonomous growth through the formation of sub-regional economic groupings. The debate on the convergence or gap between the OAU's gradualist strategy for African unity and the ECA's prescriptions for African development is outside the scope of this chapter. It is however sufficient to point out that both institutions have found enough reasons to work together towards promoting African development.

The collaboration between the OAU and ECA, especially from the late 1970s, ushered in a new phase of regional cooperation in Africa. This phase witnessed the adoption of the Monrovia Colloquium, in 1979, the Lagos Plan of Action (LPA) and the Final Act of Lagos (FLA), in 1980. These processes culminated in the signing of the Treaty establishing the African Economic Community (AEC), in 1991. In all these initiatives, the need for the development of sub-regional economic groupings was acknowledged, usually in very colourful language. The Lagos Plan of Action is easily a point of departure in the discourse on responses to the crisis of African development in general. The LPA and FAL were adopted, as blueprints for the economic and political development of Africa, by the Assembly of Heads of State and Government of the OAU, in April 1980. The Plan envisaged the formation of an African common market by the year 2000, which was to be achieved in stages; first the formation of free trade areas and, later, a common market and an economic union. The same process was to be followed in the three sub-regions identified by the Plan: Eastern and Southern Africa, Central Africa, and West Africa. It is possible that the Plan led to the establishment of the Preferential Trade Area (PTA) in Eastern and Southern Africa, which was transformed into the Common Market of Eastern and Southern Africa (COMESA), in 1993. In the West Africa sub-region, the ECOWAS that was established in 1975 predated the Plan.

Arguably, remarkable progress on African integration was made with the establishment of AEC, in June 1991, when the Abuja Treaty was signed by the OAU Heads of State and Government. The aim of the AEC was to promote economic, social and cultural development, as well as African economic integration, in order to increase self-sufficiency and endogenous development, and to create a framework for development and the mobilization of materials and human resources. The Abuja Treaty provided for the Community through a gradual process that would be achieved by coordination, harmonization, and progressive integration of the activities of existing and future regional economic communities (RECs) in Africa. The implementation of the Abuja Treaty and the establishment of the AEC were to be achieved through a six-stage process lasting 34 years. The designated starting point was the strengthening of existing RECs and creation of new ones where needed (5 years); stabilization of tariff and other barriers to regional trade and the strengthening of sectorial integration (8 years); establishment of a free trade area and a custom union in each REC (10 years); coordination and harmonization of tariffs systems among RECs, with the view to establishing an African Common Market and the adoption of common policies (4 years); and integration of all sectors, establishment of an African Central Bank and a single African currency, setting up of an African Economic and Monetary Union, and creating and electing the first Pan-African Parliament (5 years). Eight RECs that were primarily set up to promote economic integration were recognized by a decision of the AU's Assembly of Heads of State and Government, and in pursuant to the Abuja Treaty of 1991. Also, the functions of the Parliament in relation to the RECs include promoting the coordination and harmonization of policies, measures, programmes, and activities of the RECs.

The AU is the latest of Africa's broad regional integration schemes. By the close of the 1970s, it had become evident that the OAU Charter needed some amendments to enable the Organization to cope accurately with the challenges and realities of the changing world. Consequently, the Charter was amended and augmented, essentially through ad hoc decisions of the Summit, such as the Cairo Declaration Establishing the Mechanism for Conflict Prevention, Management and Resolution, etc. Even at that, it was increasingly necessary for the Organization to work towards greater efficiency. Considering some provisions of the AEC, there was urgent need to integrate the political activities of the OAU with the provisions of the AEC Treaty on economic and development issues so as to avoid duplications. Thus the Extraordinary Summit of the OAU, held in Sirte, Libya, on 9 September 1999, called for the establishment of an African Union, in conformity with the ultimate objectives of the OAU Charter and the provisions of the AEC Treaty. Following this, the Consultative Act of the African Union was adopted during the Lome Summit of the OAU, on 11 July 2000. At the 5th Extraordinary OAU/AEC Summit, held in Sirte, Libya, in March 2001, a decision declaring the establishment of the African Union, based on the unanimous will of members States, was adopted.

The relationship of AU and the RECs is regulated by the 2008 Memorandum of Understanding on Co-operation in the Area of Peace and Security, between the African Union, the Regional Economic Communities, and the Co-ordinating Mechanisms of the Regional Standby Brigades of Eastern Africa and Northern Africa. Implementation of the Memorandum is guided, inter alia, by recognition of and respect for the primary responsibility of the Union in the maintenance and promotion of peace, security, and stability in Africa, acknowledgement of the role and responsibility of the RECs in their areas of jurisdiction, and adherence to the principle of subsidiarity, complementarity, and comparative advantage (African Union 2008, Article IV). The Memorandum encourages the RECs to anticipate and prevent conflicts within and among their member states and where conflicts do occur, to undertake peacemaking and peacebuilding efforts to resolve them, including through the deployment of peace support missions. In undertaking these activities, the RECs shall keep the chairperson of the Commission fully and continuously informed (African Union 2008, Article XX). The AU is empowered to co-ordinate the harmonization of RECs and the AU views in relevant international for a, including the United Nations, and ensure that African interests and positions as defined at continental level are effectively pursued (African Union, 2008, Article XXI).

The 2008 Memorandum has been described as providing an unclear legal basis for coordination of AU and RECs activities in the peace and security arena (Striebinger, 2016). The document, however, quite clearly superimposes the AU on RECs, at least theoretically, even though, in the event of an REC refusal of AU primacy, there are no sanctions or defined lines of actions. The Memorandum does not provide details on the principles of subsidiarity, complementarity, nor comparative advantage. On some occasions, proximity of RECs to the venue of conflict, and their pre-existing relationships with parties to the conflict, might provide comparative advantage over the AU, and make the AU a "junior" and complimentary partner to the peace process. In a similar scenario, the ability of the AU to attract larger international financial and logistical support could trigger the comparative advantage principle in its favour. It would therefore be safe to assume that these principles would be driven more by politics and pragmatism than by strict legal rules. It is doubtful that the Memorandum was directly invoked and utilized in harmonizing the conflicting postures of ECOWAS and the AU in the 2010 Cote d'Ivoire crisis. The relationship between African RECs and the UN in the areas of conflict management and resolution has generally experienced some improvement since the end of the Cold War. There is still, however, room for more improvement. The AU Peace and Security Council and the Chairperson of the AU Commission have the mandate to maintain close and continued interaction with the UN Security Council and its African members, as well as with the Secretary-General, including holding periodic meetings and regular consultations on questions of peace, security, and stability in Africa (Article 17 of the PSC Protocol). On 16 November 2006, a Joint Declaration (A/61/630) on the enhancement of the UN-AU cooperation, conceived as an evolving strategic framework for UN cooperation with the AU and the regional economic communities, was signed. It was a Ten-Year Capacity-Building Program for the AU, covering: institution-building; human resources development and financial management; human rights; political, legal and electoral matters; social, economic, cultural and human development; food security; environmental protection; and, not least, peace and security (Security Council Report, 2011).

ECOWAS
15 member states

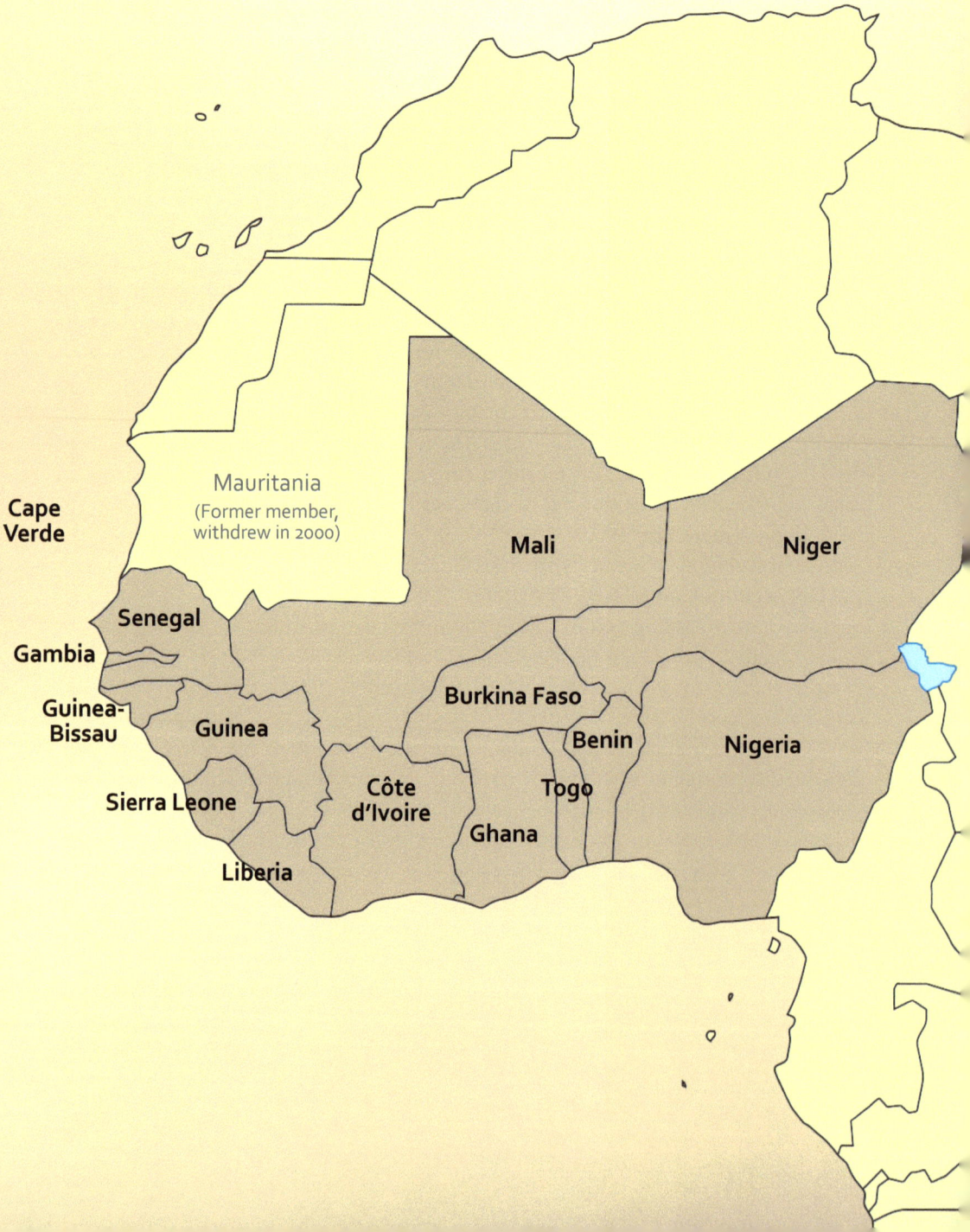

Cape
Verde

Mauritania
(Former member,
withdrew in 2000)

Mali

Niger

Senegal

Gambia

Guinea-
Bissau

Guinea

Burkina Faso

Benin

Nigeria

Sierra Leone

Côte
d'Ivoire

Togo

Ghana

Liberia

4. ECOWAS as a working peace system for West Africa

The Economic Community of West African States (ECOWAS), established in 1975 as an economic integration scheme, is the biggest regional integration scheme in West Africa. Until 1999, when Mauritania withdrew its membership, ECOWAS was made up of sixteen West African countries, including seven countries that belonged to the West African Economic and Monetary Union (UEMOA), and three countries that made up the Mano River Union (MRU). ECOWAS is the biggest of about 40 single-purpose and multi-purpose inter-governmental organisations (IGOs) that dot the West African landscape. ECOWAS was set up "to promote cooperation and development in all fields of economic activity particularly in the fields of industry, transport, telecommunications, energy, agriculture, natural resources, commerce, monetary and financial questions and in social and cultural matters for the purpose of raising the standard of living of its peoples, of increasing and maintaining economic stability, of fostering closer relations among its members and of contributing to the progress and development of the African continent" (Treaty of the Economic Community of West African States, 1975, Article 2.1). Modelled as a customs union, the ECOWAS Treaty and protocols provide a plethora of integrative instruments in the form of monetary, fiscal, administrative, institutional, and legal measures.

Although the ECOWAS Treaty (1975) was silent on conflict management and prevention, it was appreciated quiet early that no meaningful cooperation could take place within the sub-region without peace and security. The Protocol on Non-Aggression, and The Protocol Relating to Mutual Assistance on Defence, were incorporated into the ECOWAS Treaty in 1978 and 1981, respectively, to address this concern. Unfortunately, this did not prevent internal dissension, conflicts, and large scale violence in the sub-region, and it was indeed in response to these that ECOWAS came up with the idea of organised peace support operations in the region. This eventually became consolidated and codified in the 1999 Protocol on the Mechanism for Conflict Prevention, Management, Resolution, Peacekeeping and Security.

After operating the ECOWAS Treaty for almost two decades, it was found inadequate for ensuring political cooperation, regional peace, and security. The ECOWAS Revised Treaty was adopted by the Heads of State in July 1993. The Revised Treaty contains 22 chapters, divided into 93 Articles. In Article 2 of the Revised Treaty, ECOWAS "shall ultimately be the sole economic community in the region for the purpose of economic integration and the realization of the objectives of the African Economic Community." The Revised Treaty seeks to extend economic and political cooperation among member states. It designates the achievement of a common market and a single currency as economic objectives. In the political sphere, it provides for a West African Parliament, an Economic and Social Council, and an ECOWAS Court of Justice, to replace the Tribunal. The Court of Justice shall carry out the functions assigned to it and it is independent of member states and other institutions of the

Community. The judgments of the Court "shall be binding on the member states, the institutions of the Community and on individuals, and corporate bodies." The treaty also formally assigned the Community the responsibility of preventing and settling regional conflicts. Whereas it can be said that the overall logic and philosophy of ECOWAS has not changed fundamentally, it should be acknowledged that a new institutional framework was put in place under the Revised Treaty to enhance the delivery capacity of ECOWAS. The idea was to assert the supranationality of ECOWAS institutions and facilitate their functions and roles in integration processes. Also, the seemingly refreshed commitment to the ideals of democratisation and good governance informed the provision for the establishment of an ECOWAS Parliament, tailored after the European Parliament, to exercise advisory and supervisory powers over the organs of ECOWAS (Adetula, 2016).

A closer look at the Revised ECOWAS Treaty reveals the possible links to some provisions of the African Economic Community (AEC) Treaty, which regarded the African RECs as building blocks in the construction of the African Common Market. ECOWAS was designated one of the five regional pillars of the AEC. Together with The Arab Maghreb Union (AMU), the Economic Community of Central African States (ECCAS), the Common Market of Eastern and Southern Africa (COMESA), and the Southern African Development Community (SADC), ECOWAS signed the Protocol on Relations between the AEC and RECs in February 1998. The new thinking expressed in the Revised Treaty and reflected in the AU and NEPAD represent efforts to redefine regional integration more broadly, to transcend the strictly economic sphere, so as to include concerns for and consideration of peace, stability, and development. Consequently, ECOWAS is giving increased attention to issues of peace and security in West Africa.

The cornerstone of the ECOWAS legal structure for peacebuilding is Regulation MSC/REG.1/01/08, the ECOWAS Conflict Prevention Framework. Under the ECOWAS legal regime, Community laws are made through Supplementary Acts, Regulations, Directives, Decisions, Recommendations, and Opinion. The Council of Ministers enacts Regulations and Directives and makes Decisions and Recommendations. In virtue of the supranational status of ECOWAS, Regulations have general application and all their provisions are enforceable and directly applicable in Member States. They can be enforced in the institutions of the Community.[1] The ECOWAS Conflict Prevention Framework (ECPF) places primary responsibility for peace and security on ECOWAS member states. Article 7 of the ECPF declares that the ECPF is "a comprehensive operational conflict prevention and peace-building strategy that enables the ECOWAS system and member states to draw upon human and financial

---

1   The Authority passes Supplementary Acts to complete the Treaty. Decisions are enforceable in Member States and all are designated therein. Directives and their objectives are binding on all Member States. The modalities for attaining such objectives are left to the discretion of States. The Commission adopts Rules for the implementation of Acts enacted by the Council. These Rules have the same legal force as Acts enacted by the Council. The Commission makes recommendations and gives advice. Recommendations and advice are not enforceable.

resources at the regional (including civil society and the private sector) and international levels in their efforts to creatively transform conflict." It serves as a reference to strengthen human security through effective and durable cooperative interventions to prevent violent conflict and to support peacebuilding in post-conflict environments. The overall aim of the ECPF is to strengthen the human security architecture in West Africa. The intermediate purpose is to create space within the ECOWAS system, and in member states, for cooperative interaction within the region and, with external partners, to push conflict prevention and peacebuilding up the political agenda of member states, in a manner that will trigger timely and targeted multi-actor and multi-dimensional action, to defuse or eliminate potential and real threats to human security, in a predictable and institutional manner.

The ECPF presents an innovative and unique vehicle for the execution of peacebuilding activities. In theory, it is part of the laws of ECOWAS member states and therefore has the potential of resolving the contradictions inherent in the interface between peacebuilding and sovereignty. The ECPF comprises fourteen components that span the chain of initiatives designed to strengthen human security and incorporate conflict prevention activities (operational and structural), as well as aspects of peacebuilding. The components are: Early Warning; Preventive Diplomacy; Democracy and Political Governance; Human Rights and the Rule of Law; Media; Natural Resource Governance; Cross-Border Initiatives; Security Governance; Practical Disarmament; Women, Peace and Security; Youth Empowerment; ECOWAS Standby Force; Humanitarian Assistance; and Peace Education (The Culture of Peace).[2] The drafters of the ECPF found it necessary to create a separate section to establish the ECOWAS mandate and its legitimacy for conflict prevention. The ECPF incorporates the Protocol Relating to the Mechanism for Conflict Prevention, Management, Resolution, Peace-keeping and Security (1999), and the Protocol on Democracy and Good Governance (2001). It declares that "without prejudice to other regional and international legal instruments, the Mechanism and the Supplementary Protocol on Democracy and Good Governance provide the principal basis and justification for the ECPF."[3]

It is acknowledged that the ECPF provides, for the first time, a sound basis for a comprehensive peacebuilding agenda for West Africa and is also consistent with the AU's new Policy on Post-Conflict Reconstruction and Development. For the first time, ECOWAS has a framework that encompasses all the principles outlined in several normative instruments and systematically ties together the goals of conflict management, consolidation of peace, and the structural prevention of conflict to prevent the outbreak of violence and the relapse of armed conflict in societies emerging from war (Olonisakin 2011; Musah 2011; Kabia 2011). Article 53 of the Protocol Relating to the Mechanism for Conflict Prevention, Management, Resolution, Peace-Keeping and Security abrogated incompatible provisions of the 1981 ECOWAS Protocol relating to

---

2   Paragraph 42, The ECOWAS Conflict Prevention Framework.
3   Paragraph 36-39, The ECOWAS Conflict Prevention Framework.

Mutual Assistance in Defence and the 1978 Protocol on Non-Aggression. The ECPF resolved, at least theoretically, the contention between regime security and human security in favour of the latter, thereby negating the propositions that the defence and military protocols were merely "regime protection" strategies to serve the interests of ECOWAS leaders and to "insure" them against both external and internal security threats (Francis, 2009).

The objectives of the ECOWAS Vision 2020, as adopted in Abuja on 15 June 2007, are aimed at addressing four main challenges, namely:

- peacebuilding and security, promotion of the principle of good governance, and democracy;

- deepening of the integration process via the establishment of the ECOWAS common market and the interconnectivity of the markets through appropriate infrastructure;

- integration into the global economy through improved regional competitiveness, and the definition of common response strategies, in particular, as a way of addressing the different crises relating to the international economic situation; and

- pursuit of the institutional reform of the organization by providing it with resources to perform effectively and to carry out its mandate.[4]

In effect, the ECOWAS Vision 2020 sets out to replace the current "ECOWAS of States" with an "ECOWAS of People," within a strategy that sets a clear direction and goals, to enable ECOWAS to raise the standard of living of its people, and to guarantee a bright future for members in the region. The ECOWAS Vision 2020 focuses on development processes, with the people at the centre. Particularly, it desires to see a peaceful, prosperous, and cohesive region that is people-focused. The participation of the civil society is a key input in achieving the strategic vision of ECOWAS (Ajibewa, 2016).

The institutional and financial incapacity of ECOWAS poses an obstacle in realizing the aims embodied in its emerging peace and security architecture. ECOWAS has to rely on external donor support to fund its peace and security mechanism. Whilst this external support is needed to boost the capacity of ECOWAS, this risks eroding local ownership of security structures and encourages a disproportionate dependence on outside prescriptions and funding (Kabia, 2011). External actors play a dual role; on the one hand, they contribute to and strengthen the effectiveness of the ECOWAS peace and security and, on the other hand, they potentially undermine the effectiveness of the regional organization in peace and security (Francis, 2007). The real value of the ECOWAS lies in its superior knowledge of the region, deep commitment of many member states to regional security and integration, and a

---

4   See ECOWAS Commission Mid–Term Report Regional Integration as a Solution to the Global Crisis, Abuja: ECOWAS Commission, p.3).

sound normative framework that can provide the basis for systematic peace-building in the region (Olonisakin, 2011).

The ECPF is quite comprehensive, but it has been put to minimal use by ECOWAS and its member states. Several peace initiatives have been embarked upon by ECOWAS since ECPF came into effect, without any reference to the application or implementation of the framework. There needs be concerted effort towards bringing ECPF into the ECOWAS community. ECOWAS itself acknowledges the limited knowledge and limited ownership of the ECPF by member states and is actively seeking to turn the situation around (ECOWAS 2016).

Since the initial deployment of the ECOWAS Monitoring Group to Liberia, ECOWAS intervened successfully in the crises in Sierra Leone, Guinea Bissau, Cote d'Ivoire, and Mali. ECOMOG is now institutionalised as the ECOWAS Standby Force (ESF) within the framework of the AU's elaborate African Peace and Security Architecture (APSA). In this regard, ECOWAS has become an invaluable partner of the AU and by extension the UN in promoting peace and security in West Africa. An instance of such collaboration was the Africa-led International Support Mission in Mali (AFISMA), which was co-sponsored by the AU and ECOWAS. It should be recalled, however, that lack of adequate funding for the ECOWAS intervention in Mali was partly responsible for the re-hatting of AFISMA, to create the United Nations Multidimensional Stabilization Mission in Mali, MINUSMA. Notwithstanding the "success" stories about ECOWAS in conflict management in West Africa, it is plausible to argue that "the Organization literally stumbled on its peacemaking roles in the region by routinely brokering peace between its feuding leaders" (Sesay, 2016).

The development of a supranational security mechanism for conflict management and peacekeeping has progressed far more in West Africa under the Revised Treaty. ECOWAS has scaled up its normative instruments and institutional arrangements to anticipate and confront challenges to peace and security in the region, particularly with regard to conflict and political governance. The security mechanism of ECOWAS consists of a Mediation and Security Council, a Defence and Security Commission, and a Council of Elders. The Mediation and Security Council is made up of ten members, and decisions are made by a two-thirds majority of six members. It is important to note that the security mechanism of ECOWAS recognises the role of civil society in the peace process and accords it the opportunity to contribute to the organisation's early warning system mechanism. In 2008, an ECOWAS Conflict Prevention Framework (ECPF) was adopted, to guide the organisation's preventive diplomacy, which has further been strengthened by the Protocol on Democracy and Good Governance, with the provision on zero-tolerance for ascension to power through unconstitutional means. There is an ECOWAS peacekeeping mission in Guinea Bissau, ECOMIB. Also, ECOWAS is implementing a multi-million dollar defence and security sector reform programme in the country as part of the efforts to restore peace and democracy in there. The recent intervention of ECOWAS in the Malian crisis benefitted from the efficiency of the ECOWAS institutions that came with the on-going reforms. The success of the intervention by ECOWAS paved the way for the transformation of the African-led International Support Mission into the UN mission.

Arguably, the success story in the area of conflict management can be linked to the commitment of ECOWAS to good governance and democratization. It suffices to say that ECOWAS worked closely with the African Union and the United Nations to restore order and legality in member states such as Guinea, Niger, and Ivory Coast. Similarly, the same principles of ECOWAS with respect to democracy and good governance guided the stand it took on the presidential elections in Guinea, Niger, Benin, and Nigeria. The concern about the implications of the "Boko Haram" for regional security in West Africa has been expressed by ECOWAS at different levels. The ECOWAS parliament discussed the issue in one of its plenary sessions, noting that the ECOWAS and other countries within the region were already finding ways of assisting Nigeria.

The literature on the ECOWAS peacemaking activities in West Africa and the attendant challenges is very rich. However minimum attention has been given to the link between the relative successes of the ECOWAS in conflict management on the one hand and the development challenges that are confronting its member states, and for which ECOWAS was originally established. Amadu Sesay has argued that "ECOWAS has inadvertently played down the economic path to integration after it literally stumbled on its peacemaking and related activities and agenda, got stuck, to the extent that it has neglected the primary goal for which it was set up; to drive the economic integration programme of the region, grow its economy and create prosperity" (Sesay, 2016). Predictably, this has far-reaching implications for the ability of the ECOWAS member states to support the organization. In effect, "the neglect of the economic integration aspects of ECOWAS, evidenced in its failure to meet vital community targets and in particular, its inability to execute community-wide projects, has left West Africa behind other regions in economic development and human development index with negative consequences for its peacemaking efforts in the region" (Sesay, 2016).

ECOWAS has recorded significant success in managing conflicts in West Africa, through its ECPF, along with its Protocol Relating to the Mechanism for Conflict Prevention, Management, Resolution, Peace-keeping and Security 1999, and The Supplementary Protocol on Democracy and Good Governance 2001. Notwithstanding the laudable accomplishments of ECOWAS, its framework for peacebuilding is largely gender-blind in conceptualization and addresses gender concerns only superficially. The differential impact of conflicts on women and men, boys and girls is too real to be ignored. Thus, a sustainable peacebuilding system must necessarily take into account these differences. A critical review of the ECOWAS framework through a gender lens reveals the shortcomings of the framework in terms of its inability to effectively disaggregate and differentiate the problematique of violence, in terms of its implications for men and women, boys and girls (Sanda, 2016). There is a need for the ECOWAS framework to address many of the challenges facing women as a result of the power dynamics between men and women (and within gender groups) that exist at all levels of peace and conflict. In this way, peacebuilding in the ECOWAS framework is gendered. This model emphasizes the role of women in peacebuilding and peacemaking, their participation in political and decision-making, as well as the need to ensure the protection of women and other marginalized groups in conflict-affected areas (Sanda, 2016).

IGAD
8 member states

Sudan

Eritrea

Djibouti

Ethiopia

South Sudan

Somalia

Uganda

Kenya

5. IGAD peace and security initiative in the Horn of Africa

IGAD is a sub-regional organization that has the primary task of coordinating regional resource issues such as environmental degradation, draught, desertification, and deforestation, which often cause famine (IGAD 1996, Bereketeab, 2012; 173, de Klerk, 2007). It was formed in 1986 and initially known as the Inter-governmental Authority on Drought and Development (IGADD).[5] Its membership now consists of the following countries: Djibouti, Eritrea, Ethiopia, Kenya, Sudan, South Sudan, and Uganda. Eritrea suspended its membership in 2007, due to its objection to Ethiopia's invasion of Somalia, in December 2006 (Andemariam, 2015, Woodward 2013). The idea of establishing a regional organisation came from the UN, as embodied in the UN General Assembly Resolution 35/90, of December 1980 (El-Affendi, 2001, 582, Woodward 2013a). Moreover, the work of establishing the regional organisation was brought closer when the UNGA endorsed Resolution 38/216, on 20 December 1983 (Ameyo, 2010, 5). Thus, in January 1986, the Assembly of Heads of State and Government met in Djibouti and signed an agreement that formally declared the formation of IGADD (Bereketeab, 2012; 74). The UN encouraged the states of the region to establish IGADD in order to mobilise resources and capacity to combat the menace of environmental degradation: desertification, drought, and famine.

Several developments in the Horn of Africa in the early 1990s impacted the future of IGAD. The end of the Cold War engendered a new operational environment, with new actors and predispositions that had indelible impacts on IGAD and the region at large. The belligerent leaders – Gen Mohammad Siad Barre and Colonel Mengistu Hailmariam – in Somalia and Ethiopia, respectively, were deposed (Yordanov 2016, 247-8). Chaos and mayhem took hold of Somalia, while the Ethiopian People's Revolutionary Democratic Front (EPRDF) took over power in Ethiopia in, effectively, May 1991. Eritrea, after thirty years of liberation struggle, also got its independence. Upon its formal independence, in 1993, Eritrea joined IGAD. These developments no doubt introduced new issues and challenges, as well as new actors and additional momentum and dynamism into the organization. Moreover, the addition of new members also considerably galvanised the nature and functioning of the organisation. To meet the new challenges, the restructuring of IGADD and setting a different mandate were of immediate expediency. The process of restructuring was boosted by the emergence of two energetic governments with common ambition and vision. These were the EPRDF and Eritrean People's Liberation Front, the new governments in Ethiopia and Eritrea, respectively (El-Affendi 2001, 582, Mengisteab and Yohannes 200, 230). Undoubtedly, the two governments played a decisive role in pushing the restructuring work and revitalisation of IGAD.

The imperatives of post-Cold War reality also demanded new mandates for IGAD. For the first time, albeit for a brief period, the region was spared from the superpower

---

5   Preamble to the Agreement Establishing the Intergovernmental Authority on Development
     (IGAD) 1986.

rivalry that had converted it into a war theatre (Yordanov 2016, Schmidt 2013). In March 1996, the Heads of IGAD amended the organization's charter to cover political and economic issues, including conflict resolution. The relaunched IGAD was spurred by additional mandates of conflict prevention and resolution, economic cooperation and integration. Consequently, three overarching objectives were formulated: food security and environmental protection; promotion and maintenance of peace, security, and humanitarian affairs; and economic cooperation and integration (IGAD 2007a, 2010a). The attention to peace and security was indeed understandable in view of the preponderance of inter- and intra-state conflicts in the Horn of Africa. All the countries in IGAD have had significant internal security problems. There are other security concerns, such as border conflicts, pastoralist conflicts, piracy, and terrorism.

Concerned by the rampant conflicts afflicting the region, IGAD embarked on conflict prevention, management, and resolution (CPMR) initiatives (Mwaura and Schmeidl, 2002). The success of the CPMR was largely due to the early warning and response mechanism. Following its relaunch, IGAD embarked on high-profile policy issues of bilateral, regional and international magnitude and dimension. Successively, IGAD transitioned into conflict prevention, mediation, and management; peacekeeping and peacebuilding; regional integration; and migration and refugee matters (Mwaura and Schmeidl 2002, de Klerk 2007). With these efforts, IGAD made moves toward establishing a peace and security framework, with the necessary institutions and structures, in the Horn of Africa. The initial response of IGAD was to establish a peace and security division within its Secretariat, and with pressure from the international community, IGAD is according priority to issues of peace and security. IGAD operates its mandate on the prevention, management, and resolution of inter- and intra-state conflicts, essentially through the means of political dialogue, a conflict early warning system (CEWARN), and in cooperation with the AU.

The periodic summits of IGAD have provided the necessary forum for heads of state to meet and discuss conflict issues, among other things. For example, at the 1986 IGAD summit, the leaders of Ethiopia and Somalia initiated talks that eventually led to détente and the demilitarization of their borders (Deng, 1996, 137). In 1993, IGAD became involved in peace initiatives in Sudan. But the increasing partisan nature of the engagement rendered IGAD's efforts ineffective and it has been virtually comatose for three years. The resumption of the mediation with the NDA produced the Asmara Declaration, in 1995 (EL-Affendi 2001, 587). The IGAD-led peace talks resumed in 1997; Khartoum accepted the Declaration of Principles (DOP) (EL-Affendi 2001; 588, de Klerk 2007; 152). Because of perceived threats from conflicts in Somalia and Sudan, security issues received prompt attention on the agenda of IGAD, especially in the early 1990s. In 2003, the IGAD Heads of State tasked the Secretariat to develop a comprehensive peace and security strategy, thereby asserting a role for itself in the resolution of conflicts in the Horn of Africa. In April 2005, the Memorandum of Understanding and Budget for the establishment of EASBRIG were adopted.

In 2006, IGAD proposed a peace-support mission to Somalia (IGASOM), to be charged with the tasks of protecting the Somali Transnational Federal Institutions

(TFIs) and creating a conducive atmosphere for the political process. The proposal was endorsed by the AU Peace and Security Council. The UN Security Council authorized IGAD and the member states of AU to establish a protection and training mission in Somalia without an enforcement mandate for six months (Fahle, 2015). The mission, however, never took place, owing in part to the controversy over the composition of the proposed force and also to the problem of acute shortage of required technical capacity and material resources (Ibid). IGAD was also involved in peace mediation and peacebuilding processes in Sudan, Somalia, and South Sudan. It played a key role in facilitating the Comprehensive Peace Agreement, signed between the National Congress Party and Sudan People's Liberation Movement, which brought an end to one of Africa's longest running civil wars. IGAD contributed to the negotiations that culminated in the independence of South Sudan, in July 2011. IGAD mediation succeeded in Sudan because the government in Khartoum allowed it, whereas in Somalia there was no state that could either oppose or accept the IGAD's intervention. Due to international pressure and economic problems, the Bashir government conceded to the demand for the right of self-determination of south Sudanese that culminated in the independence of South Sudan (de Klerk, 2007). Apart from being involved in UN-led peace support operations in Sudan and South Sudan, IGAD has supported the African Union Mission in Somalia (AMISOM) in peacekeeping since 2007. In the remaining restive regions of Sudan, notably Darfur, Blue Nile, South Kordufan, and Kassala State, IGAD was either not involved or not successful.

IGAD was confronted with a daunting challenge in its peace mediation efforts in South Sudan. When civil war broke out on 15 December 2013, in South Sudan, IGAD was quick to respond. Ethiopia, Kenya, and Uganda, under the auspices of IGAD, took the initiative in peace brokering. Several ceasefire and peace agreements brokered by IGAD were signed, but none were implemented. The first agreement on a cessation of hostilities was signed on 23 January 2014. This was followed by the setting up of the Implementation Modality Agreement, the Monitoring and Verification Mechanism (MVM), and the Monitoring and Verification Team (MVT), to ensure implementation. Agreements were frequently violated, and deadlines were ignored by parties; consequently, peace became a remote possibility. IGAD reorganized its mediation team to IGAD-Plus, which included the UN, AU, EU, China, and representatives of the five regions of Africa. This resulted in the August 2015 Peace Agreement. Although the latter provides for a power-sharing transitional government of national unity, in July war broke out again, with dire consequences to neighbouring countries and with new rebel groups emerging (Knopf 2016). IGAD's neutrality sometimes becomes compromised, thereby making it ineligible to be a peace broker in South Sudan. IGAD's mediation in South Sudan is unravelling for reasons that include the divisiveness among IGAD member states. Neighbouring states have different agendas and are pursuing their own interests. The case of South Sudan is an example of the inability of IGAD to broker peace on its own.

IGAD performance has been hindered by the problem of over-sensitivity of members on sovereignty and internal affairs, which in addition to unhealthy rivalry and competition among member states makes it difficult to have broad-based consensus. For instance, there is the long-unsettled border conflict between Ethiopia and Eritrea. The latter suspended its membership of the IGAD to avoid participation in any military intervention in Somalia. Neither Sudan nor Ethiopia has demonstrated actual or potential attributes of a "core state," which would lead them to assume leadership responsibility within IGAD, as both countries have overwhelming domestic challenges. While IGAD's CEWARN is seen as functioning, its limited coverage and lack of capacity to monitor conflict indicators across the entire sub-region is a major limitation. Closely related to this is the lack of enforcement of IGAD resolutions against member states, especially on the outbreak of conflict and humanitarian emergencies (Hull et al, 2011, 9). Apart from these, the IGAD is confronted with the problem of funds. None of the member states is rich enough to provide support in the way Nigeria supported the ECOMOG operations in Liberia and Sierra Leone. Hence, the accomplishments of the IGAD have remained quite marginal, compared with ECOWAS.

Notwithstanding its challenges, IGAD has engaged in complex reconciliation work in the region, and cooperates closely with the AU Peace and Security Architecture. The IGAD region suffers from multiple interconnected pathologies that include intra-state insurgencies in Ethiopia, Sudan, Uganda, and Somalia; inter-state conflicts between Somalia and Ethiopia, Sudan-Ethiopia, Sudan-Uganda, Sudan-South Sudan, Ethiopia-Eritrea, and Eritrea-Djibouti; and environmental degradation, droughts and famine, international intervention, and underdevelopment. These pathologies feed into each other, making the Horn of Africa the most conflict-ridden region on the African continent and, arguably, in the world (Woodward 2013, Cliffe 1999, Mengisteab 2014, de Klerk 2007). During its history, IGAD faced conflicts affecting virtually all member states and quite frequently IGAD's response has been neither adequate, balanced, impartial, comprehensive, nor holistic.

IGAD lacks a comprehensive peace and security policy framework to adequately address the peace and security challenges of the region. In the absence of a comprehensive policy framework, these challenges are denied their proper context and are treated as appendages of global problems, embedded within overall security concerns as international terrorism, piracy, and the scramble for resources (Rotberg, 2005). This situation logically renders the IGAD states into mere allies and non-allies that protect and advance the geo-strategic interests of the global powers and their regional surrogates. A good illustration was the invasion by Kenya and Ethiopia of Somalia, and Uganda's involvement in the South Sudan civil war (Apuuli 2015). This explains the prominence of the Conflict Early Warning and Response Mechanism (CEWARN) and the Capacity Building Programme Against Terrorism (ICPAT) in the programmes devised by IGAD and its friends to enforce peace and security in the Horn. It should be stated that the use of CEWARN as early warning for potential conflicts has recorded only limited success in cross-border pastoralist conflicts (Mengisteab, 2014, 198).

In January 2016, IGAD commemorated its 30th anniversary. Thirty years in the life of an organisation might not be considered as long enough for judgement, but compared with other African RECs, IGAD is often seen as weak. At least four factors are presumed to account for the weakness. The first concerns the structure of IGAD, while the second relates to its dependence on external financing. The third concerns the dearth of capacity, which undermines IGAD's operations, efficacy, and performance. A fourth factor contributing to the weakness is Ethiopia's dominance, and controversial role, in IGAD. It is contentious whether the status and role of Ethiopia as a regional power has added value to the process and outcome of regional integration and development in the Horn of Africa. There is a widespread perception in the Horn of Africa that Ethiopia is systematically exploiting the IGAD for its own narrow interests. For example, in December 2006, Ethiopia invaded Somalia and vanquished the Islamic Courts Union (ICU), and convinced IGAD to retroactively legitimise this invasion. To many Somalis, this invasion was simply a continuation of the perennial Ethiopian hostility, intended to weaken Somalia (Samatar, 2013). The action certainly eroded trust in IGAD among Somalis. The invasion was also Eritrea's reason for suspending its membership in IGAD (Andemaria 2015, de Waal 2015, Mengisteab 2014). Similarly, IGAD's failure to take up the Eritrea Ethiopia conflict can be regarded as an indication of the Ethiopian grip on the organisation (Mengisteab 2014).

It seems that other member states have acquiesced, either willingly or by compulsion, to the Ethiopian dominance of IGAD. Roughly speaking, there have been two sorts of "natural" alignment within the IGAD. One group consists of Ethiopia, Kenya, and Uganda, while another consists of Sudan, Eritrea, Djibouti, and Somalia. The first group is considered as allied to the West and, of course, as trusted partners in the global war on terror (GWAT). The first group, and indeed the West, see the second group as being part of the weak link in the GWAT. Also, members of second group face serious problems that make their inner unity precarious. Somalia has no properly functioning state, while Djibouti is completely controlled by Ethiopia and Western powers, particularly the US. Ethiopia has already succeeded in neutralising Eritrea, effectively barring it from IGAD, and placing it under UN sanctions and diplomatic isolation. Also, the civil war in South Sudan has created a serious rift between Ethiopia and Uganda, wherein Uganda has begun seriously challenging Ethiopia's dominance. The government of Salva Kiir perceives Ethiopia as siding with opposition led by Riek Machar, and that puts a wedge in the relation between South Sudan and Ethiopia. Recently, however, Ethiopia seems to have undergone a ninety-degree swing and is trying to isolate Riek Machar.

Since 2008, in contravention of its statute, Ethiopia holds the position of chairmanship of IGAD. Ethiopia's tactic for holding on to the chairmanship has been by holding only extraordinary meetings. Convening an ordinary meeting would have set a different meeting agenda, so that Ethiopia would have been compelled to surrender not only the chairmanship of the IGAD to the next country in line, but also to reactivate Eritrea's membership.[6] Since 2011, Eritrea has been trying to reactivate its membership, but it has been blocked (Andemariam, 2015, 1) by Ethiopia. The dominance of IGAD by Ethiopia is having its toll on the organisation. The unity of IGAD

6   Interview with the staff of the IGAD Secretariat, in February 2016, Djibouti.

is adversely affected. According to a member of the staff of the IGAD Secretariat, in Djibouti, all member countries of IGAD, except Ethiopia and Kenya, have ceased paying their membership dues, possibly in reaction to their perception of Ethiopia's dominance.[7]

The Agreement Establishing the Intergovernmental Authority on Development underscores the importance of the principle of non-interference in the internal affairs of Member States. Thus, the management of inter- and intra-state conflict is essentially limited to dialogue and moral persuasion. In this regard, the principles and strategies for managing conflict, as provided in Article VI of the IGAD Agreement, are patterned after the OAU model, which is now outdated. The IGAD principles of non-interference, and of the resolution of inter- and intra-state conflict through dialogue only, stand in conflict with the AU Constitutive Act that is designed to meet contemporary challenges of peace and security on the African continent.

IGAD's performance is further hampered by the pre-eminence of personality over institutions in operations of the organization. The defective institutional setup within IGAD creates challenges for its ability to function. Not only is the peace and security framework state-centric, its processes are driven by the interests of Ethiopia, its largest contributor and most influential member (Ajibewa, 2016). The organization is only strong and effective on issues that the leadership and governments of the member states allow it to be. For example, it is able to be involved in peace mediation in member states only when and if the member states concerned are willing. The strong inclination to allot absolute power to national political leaders explains the frequent paralysis IGAD suffers. In effect, the organisation's performance is largely dependent on warm and cordial personal relationships among the leaders of IGAD member states. Many have come to regard IGAD as a club of Heads of State and Government. This "top-bottom" approach has remained pervasive in IGAD, and it endows the Assembly of Heads of State and Government absolute power over the citizens whose interests and needs should determine the course and direction of IGAD operations. The reason for the poor performance of CEWARN in dealing with the "hard conflict" between states is the inter-state nature of IGAD, where a state could block an action if it goes against the personal interests of its leader (de Klerk 2007). Within this setting, there are limited opportunities for citizens' participation in the various aspects of regional integration, including the promotion of peace and regional security.

IGAD's dependence on external funding for its core activities is a major limitation. In 1994, an international donor group – "Friends of IGADD," consisting of Italy, Canada, the UK, the Netherlands, Norway, and the United States – was formed, to enhance the international profile of IGAD. The Friends of IGAD pledged to contribute to the promotion of IGADD's efforts in peacemaking and regional integration (El-Affendi, 2001, 583). Following the restructuring into IGAD, "Friends of IGADD" was transformed into the "IGAD Partners Forum" (IPF), assuming more formal roles (EL-Affendi, 2001, 584; de Klerk 2007, 148). Today, the main funders of IGAD pro-

---

7   Interview with the staff of the IGAD Secretariat, in February 2016, Djibouti.

jects and peace operations are the United States, the United Kingdom, the European Union, Turkey, and the United Arab Emirates. CEWARN remains heavily reliant on donor funds. Also, the CSOs Forum has been inactive, due to lack of funds, especially since GIZ stopped providing funding for its activities (Ajibewa, 2016). Resource constraints also impacts development of the Organization's human resources (Woodward 2013, 176).

The strong presence of IPF in the commemoration of the 30th Anniversary of IGAD was a clear indication of the dominant influence of external actors in the affairs of the organisation. External donors do more than simply inform the activities of IGAD. Indeed, some have argued that IGAD has simply become the effectuator of the foreign policy wishes of its funders. As Mengisteab (2014, 147) relays, "in large part, due to its excessive dependence on external financing of its operations, IGAD has largely become a conduit for external influence on the region rather than an agent for sheltering the region from external meddling." This over-involvement of external actors deprives the regional organisation of the domestic legitimacy that it crucially needs. It also affects the sustainability, integrity, and clarity of the projects initiated and funded by external actors. A good example of this is the gradual crumbling of the IGAD/AU peace mission in Somalia, owing in part to the 20 percent reduction of EU's contribution to the mission, which in turn has made Ethiopia begin the withdrawal of its forces. It is possible that Uganda, Kenya, and Burundi will follow the same path soon.

Challenges and Opportunities for Improved Performance

Where sub-regional mechanisms for conflict management have recorded appreciable success, such as in the case of ECOWAS/ECOMOG, in West Africa, it is arguably the result of paying attention to issues of good governance and democratization. Amadu Sesay argues that the sub-regional groupings that have enjoyed relative success stress the central role of democratization and good governance in their programmes of conflict management and resolution (Sesay, 2002). Some of the principles espoused in the Revised Treaty of the Economic Community of West African States and other major declarations on the various conflicts in West Africa underline the notion that democratization, coupled with responsive and responsible governance, is the most effective conflict management tool. In contrast, it has been difficult to get member states of IGAD to agree on some governance-related issues, as well as on the logic of and approaches to conflict management mechanisms in the Horn of Africa. IGAD illustrates a case of lack of consensus among member states.

Unlike the seemingly ideological neutrality of relief operations, the task of peacebuilding and reconstruction is as openly political as that of development, carrying with it certain assumptions about the primacy of particular norms, values, and institutions. (Rugumamu 2009). It should be obvious to all concerned – but alas, it is not – that the sole agenda around which everyone should unite in a post-conflict situation can only be one that serves the interest of the people we pretend to be there to help, and they alone. The reality, however, is that there invariably is a plurality of different agendas and if the national interest of the local population is not totally ignored, it is rarely given the priority it deserves. Even the United Nations and its agencies are all too often guilty of giving too much importance to considerations of prestige and their own funding needs, at the expense of what is actually required to establish and consolidate peace and stability (Brahimi 2007; Francis 2009).

The United Nations Peacebuilding Commission is activated primarily on request from the UNSC, or from the state in question. While this may appear to be a legally safe formality, it does not guarantee that the programs and activities of peacebuilding will not infringe on the sovereignty of the recipient State. The first task for the international community, when it engages in a peace operation, should be the establishment of a solid partnership with the national stakeholders. In that partnership, the leadership role of the nationals must be unquestionably recognized. The foreigners need to fully understand and accept that, vital as their own contributions may be, this is not their country, their stay is temporary, and however important and even indispensable their contribution – security forces, financial aid, and technical expertise – might be, they do not have the right to impose their views over the national will and the legitimate aspirations of the indigenous people. To underscore the primacy of local over foreign concerns in no way means that the international partners have to accept the views of the local parties unconditionally and without discussion (Brahimi 2007).

The interface of sovereignty with peacebuilding by external actors is slippery terrain. In response to the myriad problems of desecrating the sovereignty of host nations of peacebuilding activities, the AU stipulates national and local ownership of peacebuilding processes as a cardinal principle of its peacebuilding architecture. Paragraph 17 of the African Union Policy on Post-Conflict Reconstruction and Development provides that the principle of national and local ownership is critical to ensure that PCRD activities are aligned to local needs and aspirations; enhance a common understanding of a shared vision; maximize support for PCRD through the engagement/ re-engagement of the population in their governance, and guarantee sustainability of recovery efforts. The six pillars upon which all PCRD efforts should be developed and sustained across the different phases of action are; a) security; b) humanitarian/emergency assistance; c) political governance and transition; d) socio-economic reconstruction and development; e) human rights, justice, and reconciliation; and f) women and gender. Intervention in these areas places the external actor right at the heart of critical domestic issues that ordinarily are shut out of the view of non-locals (Jaiyebo and Adetula 2016)

At the United Nations level, it has been canvassed that in the aftermath of violence, neither a cohesive nation state, nor an inclusive system of governance, can be taken for granted. The national responsibility to drive efforts to sustain peace must therefore be broadly shared across all key social strata and divides. A wide spectrum of political opinions and national actors, in particular women and young people, must be heard. Sustaining peace, which fundamentally concerns reconciliation and building a common vision of a society, must be understood as a task that only national stakeholders can undertake. The United Nations and international actors can accompany and facilitate the process, but not lead it. It should also accord priority support to broadening inclusion so that peacebuilding processes are nationally owned in the fullest sense (United Nations 2015). It must be mentioned that Security Council Resolution 2282 (2016) reaffirmed the need for national ownership of peacebuilding efforts, and urged the Peacebuilding Commission to hold regular exchanges of views with relevant regional and sub-regional organizations.

Between the AU and RECs there are a number of instruments to promote constitutionalism and democratization on the continent. This is important, especially for a continent where a significant percentage of its armed conflicts are traceable to issues that relate to constitutional matters such as forceful change of governments, military coups, election cancelations, etc. Interestingly, the AU was able to respond to these challenges from the outset by making sure that the Constitutive Act prohibits any member state that undergoes an unconstitutional transfer of power from participating in the activities of the Union. With this principle in place, the AU has been able to condemn military takeovers and also initiate transitions to democracy in some African countries. African RECs, notably ECOWAS and the SADC, have been assisted in ensuring free and fair elections in some countries in their respective regions, both at the level of election monitoring, and in mediation to help resolve electoral conflicts. These demonstrable changes in the commitment to constitutionalism have been expressed by ECOWAS in its Protocol on Good Governance, which it has enforced against unconstitutional regimes in West Africa with varying degrees of success.

The involvement and participation of the citizens in regional integration processes must be encouraged by the RECs. A survey conducted in fifteen African countries between 2002 and 2003 shows that only 49 per cent of the respondents have heard of continental bodies such as the African Union (even when referred to in the questionnaire by its former name, the OAU), or the regional economic community of their own region, whether the SADC, EAC, or ECOWAS (Afrobarometer, 2003). The consequence for the execution of regional programmes and collective security initiatives, including peace support operations, is the risk of a lack of domestic support in many African countries. A case in point is Nigeria's continuous generous support for the ECOWAS peacekeeping operations in West Africa. While Nigeria has made significant contributions towards regional peace and security in West Africa, at home, successive Nigerian governments have been criticized in the media for unjustified investments in the ECOWAS peace support operations. A section of the Nigerian foreign policy community feels that Nigeria has not been duly acknowledged for its roles in promoting peace and security in West Africa.

The complicity of state and non-state actors in conflicts within a region is a serious challenge, especially in cases where national and regional actors are either inclined towards parochial nationalism or are interested parties in the conflicts. In some instances, the problem is how to contain unhealthy rivalry among states within the region, or how to manage changes in the regional balance of power in the aftermath of intervention. Unhealthy rivalries among member states of IGAD provide us with useful illustrations. There is also the challenge of how to check the expansionist aspirations of some regional powers that want to exploit conflict situations to their advantage. Regional powers, notably Ethiopia, South Africa, and Nigeria, have come under the watchful eyes of other countries with which they share membership of RECs, often because of the unsubstantiated claim that they have imperial ambitions.

Also, lack of consensus among the states in the sub-region creates difficulties. For example, Nigeria initially faced opposition from Ivory Coast and a few other member states of ECOWAS over the legality of ECOMOG intervention in Liberia. More recently, ECOWAS countries were divided on whether the sub-regional body should intervene in the conflict in Ivory Coast. Nigeria and Ghana had contrary views on this matter. While Nigeria was in support of intervention, Ghana openly expressed unwillingness to deploy troops to Ivory Coast. The inability to act in a unified manner was a major hindrance to the resolution of the conflict in Ivory Coast. In East Africa, Ethiopia's and Kenya's interventions in Somalia in 2006 and 2011, respectively, were deeply problematic and had less to do with stabilizing that country and more about the promotion of national interests. The AU proposed that the neighbouring countries with interests in Somalia should not be part of the AU initiative. The strategy was abandoned, however, when the AU and UN agreed to make the Kenyan troops already in Somalia part of AMISOM. The efforts by IGAD to mediate in the conflict between the government of South Sudan and armed opposition were unsuccessful partly because of the complicity of some countries in the Horn of Africa.

Conclusions, policy recommendations, and research priorities

The increased role of Africa's RECs in conflict management, peacekeeping, and peacebuilding is an important feature of the emerging post-Cold War system. ECOWAS, IGAD, and other RECs in Africa will continue to be relevant in this regard. In strengthening the capacity of the RECs to effectively address the peacebuilding challenges facing Africa, there is a need to pay attention to experience-sharing among the regional institutions, in order to enhance their capacities to effectively design and implement regional peacekeeping programmes in their respective regions. There have been efforts to facilitate intra-Regional Economic Communities collaboration over the past decade. In 2008, the Geneva-based Centre for Humanitarian Dialogue (HD) facilitated a Working Exchange between ECOWAS and IGAD, with a focus on peace and security matters. This resulted in exchanges of visits by both organizations to gain insight into the workings of their respective peace and security architectures (Ajibewa, 2016). The United Nations Office of the Special Adviser for Africa (OSAA) and the AU have intensified their effort towards institutionalizing cooperation among RECs, and support them in moving towards the implementation of global and continental development frameworks. The frequent exchange of ideas and progress reports on the implementation of the United Nations Sustainable Development Goals (SDGs) and the AU Agenda 2063, have become a norm among the RECs on the AU platform. This relatively new collaboration among RECs will prove useful in its efforts to strengthen the peace and security architectures of the existing RECs (Ajibewa, 2016).

Africa's regional institutions have made appreciable progress in promoting peace in Africa. However, there are challenges to be addressed, among which is the need to strengthen the legal and institutional frameworks in order to support regional collective security, clarify roles, and guide the harmonization of the existing peacebuilding strategies and programmes. Far more than IGAD, both ECOWAS and the AU have considerably elaborate provisions for peace and security that cover the entire field from prevention to post-conflict development. However, the post-conflict recovery and development components require significant improvement. For example, the practice of deploying military forces to make or enforce peace and then walking away, leaving external actors to do post-conflict recovery and development, must be discouraged.

The need for the involvement of civil society in regional peacebuilding activities and programmes cannot be over-emphasised. Also, the development and growth of transnational civil society at the regional level, through networks of civil society groups across national borders, should be encouraged. Such platforms can be used to promote Pan-African cooperation that will support the collective regional security through peace education and other forms of civic engagements. At the global level, the engagement of African regional organizations with international institutions, on how to consolidate the regionalist approach to peace and security in Africa, should be encouraged. The efforts made by the United Nations and its various agencies are commendable and their sustainability should be encouraged. With respect to peace processes, civil society involvement helps to bring a broad range of social and political interests to the negotiating table, making a process more inclusive and participatory. Citizen groups tend to have direct communication channels with community leaders of aggrieved constituencies and can conduct back-channel, bottom-up discussions to encourage disaffected groups to seek political solutions. The participation of civil society enhances the legitimacy of the reconciliation process, builds social consensus around the terms of an accord, and helps to hold political elites accountable to their promised agreements (Kroc Institute for International Peace Studies, 2014).

In many post-recovery situations, the local populations are ignored in the planning and implementation of intervention programmes and activities, while the space is dominated by the "armies of consultants and non-governmental organizations" that often arrive with "readymade" solutions. The emerging danger is the increasing access given to local and international non-government organizations without corresponding mechanisms for accountability. If the trend is left unchecked, the emerging scenario might be either imperialism of international NGOs, or the tyranny of local NGOs.

The Constitutive Act supports engagement with African non-state institutions in resolving African conflicts. This no doubt suggests that civil society has an important role to play in shaping peace and security policies and processes in Africa. Without sufficient participation of civil society groups, either in the political process where decisions relating to regional cooperation and integration programmes are taken, or through adequate consultation, efforts and initiatives stand the risk of becoming easy prey for sabotage. There are also increasing opportunities in Africa for civil society to engage in peace and security issues. However, African CSOs generally lack the technical capacity and experience to engage in peace and security issues effectively. First, the civil society organizations lack the necessary resource base and organizational capacity to effectively engage government and other stakeholders. Secondly, many African governments, for their part, have become increasingly intolerant of civil society organizations, especially on the matter of peace and security. Civil society organizations do not have access to information about security. This has negative consequences for an increased role for civil society. It is encouraging to note that there are new initiatives within the NEPAD and the AU to help develop the capacities of Africa CSOs. These initiatives need to be translated into concrete agendas and programmes for civil society engagement with the structures and processes of regional collective security in Africa.

International and domestic non-governmental organizations are a growing force in contemporary international relations. The relationship, in early warning, between the ECOWAS and the West Africa Network for Peacebuilding (WANEP), is an example of a unique "partnership to serve the people." ECOWARN provides daily assessments of conflict-related trends across its fifteen member states. It draws on the knowledge and analysis of a pool of civil society actors from WANEP and government-appointed observers from each member state. The ECOWAS relationship with civil society has helped inform its interventions on multiple occasions. WANEP policy briefs helped ECOWAS play an effective mediation role in Guinea in 2007. In Cote D'Ivoire, WANEP recommendations about direct dialogue led to the Ouagadougou accords (Kabia 2011). IGAD's own early warning system, CEWARN, draws on local networks to collect information on cross-border and pastoral conflicts in the Horn of Africa and is considered one of its most successful programs (Kroc Institute for International Peace Studies, 2014).

A strong resource base is indispensable for successful and sustainable peacebuilding initiatives in the region. Inadequate funding for ECOWAS peacebuilding intervention and related activities is a serious challenge. The Mali-After-Action Review of ECOWAS Initiatives and Responses to the Multidimensional Crises in Mali, November 2013 to February 2014, boldly revealed that "ECOWAS lacks the requisite strategic, military, logistical and financial base for autonomous action during violent conflicts in a non-permissive environment" (2014, 25). The poor state of financial resources due to non-commitment of member states to their financial obligations has made ECOWAS and IGAD more vulnerable and susceptible to manipulation by external forces, which in turn affects the autonomy and performance of the two bodies. Africa RECs and the AU are supranational organizations and African leaders should mobilize the needed resources at home and abroad to live up to the expectations of the charters of the respective organizations. It is yet to be seen how ECOWAS and the AU will respond to the breakdown of law and order that is not connected to elections nor unconstitutional take-over of government. Also, when engaged in peacekeeping operations, ECOWAS should stay engaged through the entire continuum of peacebuilding in execution of its delegated powers under the ECPF. In order to enhance coordination at the various levels, there is a need for effective liaison offices to be established in ECOWAS and IGAD, to interface with the United Nations Peacebuilding Commission Configuration Committee of UN-PBC focus countries, in their respective jurisdictions.

The organizational and decision-making capabilities necessary for effective management of peace support processes and operations are still not adequately available within the AU and the RECs. For instance, the nature of African conflicts requires conflict resolution strategies and operations that come with a reasonable level of authority. Similarly, the power to enforce sanctions and ensure compliance with resolutions and decisions is very necessary. Also, prevention of violent conflicts requires technical capacity for pre-emptive intervention, especially at the earlier stages of conflicts.

Global developments and trends have far-reaching implications for the principles and practice of peacebuilding. More than ever, peace and development are now more intimately linked and are often regarded by many, including the UN and other international actors, as inseparable goals. This has significantly influenced the emergence of new conceptions about peace, security, and development. However, there is need for further reflection on the peace-development nexus in a way that pays attention to the link between conflict and global development. Tilma Bruck has helped draw attention to the unwarranted "silence on security, conflict and peace in the global development." He observed that "none of the Millennium Development Goals (MDGs) refers to peace or security (2013, 1). Arguably, the United Nations Sustainable Development Goals (SDGs) include components that seek to address gaps in previous global and regional development initiatives, such as the Millennium Development Goals (MDGs), and it is expected that Africans RECs, AU, and NEPAD will buy into the new orientation by developing frameworks and indicators that relate peace and security to development goals. For example, it should be possible to broaden the existing governance indicators, within the framework of the Peer Review Mechanism of the AU/NEPAD, to include indicators and parameters that define and measure the dimensions of armed conflicts and appropriately project them as threats and risk factors for development processes and outcomes. In this way, targets and benchmarks for peace and security can be developed to guide states and regional actors. Also, this approach calls for mainstreaming conflict prevention analysis at all levels of development planning and implementation – national, regional, and global (Adetula, 2015a).

The challenge of governance in Africa is evident in the negative development indicators, such as the problems of massive unemployment and illiteracy. The 2015 Mo Ibrahim governance index clearly shows that democratic institutions and governance systems in many countries in Africa are weak or non-existent. The Protocol on Democracy and Good Governance, 2001, was indeed a response to this trend. There is a need to promote new thinking within the RECs, thinking that measures good governance in terms of effective and efficient delivery of public goods and services to the majority of the citizens. Beyond the efforts of individual African governments to address the need for good governance, there should be a regional strategy on how to promote it. Good governance can significantly reduce the incidence of violent conflict in Africa.

Pre-violent conflict or post-conflict peacebuilding is essentially a response to failure of government at critical levels. At its very essence, there is an appropriation and deployment of sovereign powers. It is a fine line between augmenting government failure through peacebuilding, and usurpation of a country's sovereignty. By their very nature, peacebuilding processes pertain to matters that ordinarily should be within the exclusive preserve of a nation state. When states are in the immediate post-conflict stage, with the national economy in shambles, and law and order maintainable only with the assistance of external actors, pragmatism drives questions of sovereignty to the rear. With the leaders and government in a state of extreme vulnerability, the only restraint on external actors is their own sense of self-restraint.

The importance of the global context cannot be overemphasized. The international environment provides opportunities and as well poses some challenges to RECs. International partners who can be considered "friends of the continent" are responding positively by supporting African regional and sub-regional organizations in promoting the regionalist approach to conflict resolution. The adoption of the G8 Africa Action Plan at Kananaskis, in 2002, was remarkable in this regard. It set out comprehensive G8 commitments with a focus on peace support operations in Africa. Also, within the framework of the EU Strategy for Africa, the EU members have funded the implementation of the European Security and Defence Action Plan, to support peace and security in Africa. Support from some of the new global powers has also gone to the AU mechanisms for peace and stability, but they have shown less interest in the sub-regional organizations. The international community should broaden its notion of preventive diplomacy to include consideration of support to Africa in addressing new forms of violence in the region, through support for the development of comprehensive early warning systems at both national and regional levels.

The prospects of RECs in Africa, in the performance of their expanded mandates, will depend on developments within the RECs themselves, as well as the dynamics in Africa, and some global developments. This has several political ramifications that demand complex institutions and structures, and extensive political will, as well as unity of objectives and commitments at national, sub-regional, and continental levels. It suffices to say that the successful development and deployment of RECs in effectively and efficiently undertaking peacebuilding activities in Africa will depend first on the commitment of African states to redefining regional integration in a way that de-emphasises the state-centred approaches in favour of one that is people-centred .

Further research is required in order to examine the processes and outcomes of the engagement of RECs with peacebuilding in other sub-regions, notably North Africa and Central Africa; and the perceptions and assessments of citizens on the performance of RECs in peacebuilding and others aspects of conflict management. The roles and responsibilities of national, regional, and other actors in peacebuilding need to be studied in a more elaborate way if the logic of interests underlying behaviour of these actors is to be understood. Such knowledge is also useful for understanding, for instance, the complicity of some actors (national, regional, and global) in some of the violent conflicts in Africa. Other areas for further research include the political economy of peace support operations in Africa, and the involvement of the business community, including the organized private sector, in peacebuilding in Africa. For example, while the impacts of civil wars in Africa are becoming popular research subjects, the role of the business community often remains undocumented. Similarly, new research initiatives on transnational civil society and peacebuilding are needed to guide RECs and other inter-governmental agencies.

References

Adetula, V (2016) "Regional Organizations, Public Goods, and the Re-Conceptualization of Peace-building in Africa" Paper presented at the Policy Dialogue on Regional Economic Communities and Peace Building in Africa, Institute for Peace and Conflict Resolution, IPCR, Abuja 1-2 September, and Abuja.

Adetula, V (2008) "The role of sub-regional integration schemes in conflict prevention & management in Africa; A framework for working peace system" in Alfred Nhema & Paul Zeleza (eds.) The resolution of African conflicts; The management of conflict resolution and post conflict reconstruction, OSSREA/James Currey/UNISA Press/ Ohio University Press pp.9-21.

Adetula, V (2005) "Development, conflict and peacebuilding in Africa" in Shedrack Gaya Best (ed.) Introduction to peace and conflict studies in West Africa University for Peace/ Spectrum Books Ltd. 2005, pp.383-405.

Adetula, V (2003) "Economic and socio-cultural networks in West Africa: What prospects for the development of transnational civil society?" in Civil society partners for democracy; ICSF-2003 Documents, Ulaanbaatar, Mongolia; ICSF pp.136-142.

Adetula, V (2015a) African Conflicts, Development, and Regional Organisations in the Post-Cold War International System Current Issues 61, Afrikainstitut Uppsala,

Adetula, V (2015b) "Globalization and its Consequences for Africa's Security and Development", in Amadu Sesay and Charles Ukeje (eds.) Security and Developmental Challenges for Africa in the 21st Century, Kuru, National Institute for Policy and Strategic Studies, pp. 157-180.

African Union (2008) Memorandum of Understanding on Co-operation in the Area of Peace and Security between the African Union, the Regional Economic Communities and the Co-ordinating Mechanisms of the Regional Standby Brigades of Eastern Africa and Northern Africa: AU Commission

African Union (2010) African peace and security architecture (APSA): 2010 Assessment Study Addis Ababa:

Afrobarometer (2003) "Africans' Views of International Organizations" Afrobarometer Briefing Paper No. 8 August 2003.

Ajibewa, R (2016) "Towards a Human Security-centred Approach to Regional Peacebuilding: ECOWAS' Experiences and Lessons for IGAD'" Paper presented at the Policy Dialogue on Regional Economic Communities and Peace Building in Africa, Institute for Peace and Conflict Resolution, IPCR, Abuja 1-2 September, and Abuja.

Ameyo, D. K (2010) "Study on the Comprehensive Review of the Agreement Establishing the Intergovernmental Authority on Development (IGAD)" Unpublished paper.

Andemariam, S W. 2015. "In, Out or at the Gate? The Predicament on Eritrea's Membership and Participation Status in IGAD", Journal of African Law, 59(2), pp. 355–379. doi: 10.1017/S0021855315000091.Accesses 2nd January 2017.

Asante, S.K.B.(2004)"The Travails of Integration" in Adebajo & Ismail, (eds.) West Africa's Security Challenges; Building Peace in a Troubled Region, Boulder & London; Lynne Rienner,

Ascher, W and Mirovitskaya, N. (2013) "Development strategies and the evolution of violence in Africd4a" in Ascher, W and Mirovitskaya, N. (eds.) The economic roots of conflict and cooperation in Africa Palgrave Macmillan.

Bam, S (2012) "Foreword" in Linnea Gelot et al (eds.) Supporting African Peace Operations Policy Dialogue No. 8, The Nordic Africa Institute, pp. 8-9.

Bereketeab, Redie (2016) "Peace Building in Africa: Popular Progressive versus Neoliberal Peace Building" Paper presented at the Policy Dialogue on Regional Economic Communities and Peace Building in Africa, Institute for Peace and Conflict Resolution, IPCR, Abuja 1-2 September, and Abuja.

Bereketeab, Redie. 2012. "Inter-Governmental Authority on Development (IGAD); A Critical Analysis", in Kidane Mengisteab and Redie Bereketeab (eds.), Regional Integration, Identity and Citizenship in the Greater Horn of Africa. Woodbridge and Rochester; James Currey

Bereketeab, Redie. 2014. 'The Challenges of Regional Integration in the Horn of Africa', Journal of US-China Public Administration, Vol. 11, No. 5, pp. 401-414

Brahimi L (2007) "State Building in Crisis and Post Conflict Countries", Paper delivered at the Seventh Global Forum on Reinventing Government Building Trust in Government 26-29 June 2007, Vienna, Austria

Brewer, J (2010) Peace processes; a sociological approach Wiley, John & Sons, Inc.

Bruck, T (2013) "An economist's perspective on security, conflict and peace research" in SIPRI Yearbook 2013; Armaments, disarmament and international security Oxford University Press.

Chesterman S (2005) "From State Failure to State-Building; Problems and Prospects for a United Nations Peacebuilding Commission" Journal of International Law and International Relations Vol. 2 No 1 winter pp. 155 – 175

Daniel, D, Hayes, B, and Oudraat, C (1998) Coercive inducement and the containment of international crises Washington, DC; U.S. Institute of Peace Press.

De Klerk, Britt. 2007. 'Navigating Conflict Management; The Case of IGAD in the Horn of Africa', in Korwa G. Adar and Peter J. Schraeder (eds.), Globalisation and Emerging Trends in African Foreign Policy, Volume II; A Comparative Perspective of Eastern Africa. Lanham, Boulder, New York, Toronto, Plymouth, UK; University Press of America

De Waal, A (2013) "Syria; a view from Africa" http;//africanarguments.org/2013/09/12/syria-a-view-from-africa-by-alex-de-waal/ (Accessed on 15/01/14).

Deng, F (1996) Sovereignty as responsibility; Conflict management in Africa, Washington DC; The Brookings Institution.

ECOWAS (2006) Supplementary Protocol A/SP.1/06/06 Amending the Revised ECOWAS Treaty

ECOWAS (2008) The ECOWAS Conflict Prevention Framework ECOWAS MSC/ REG.1/01/08

ECOWAS (2016) Opening remarks by the ECOWAS Commissioner for Political Affairs, Peace and Security (PAPS) Mrs. Halima Ahmed at the two-Day sensitization Workshop on the 29th of August 2016 www.ecowas.int Accessed on 1 September, 2016

El-Affendi, Abdelwahab (2001)'The Impasse in the IGAD Peace Process for Sudan; The Limits of Regional Peacemaking?' African Affairs, Vol. 100, no. 401, pp. 581-99

Fahle, F (2015) "The African Union mission in Somali; Toward a new vision of regional peace keeping" Peter Wallensteen and Anders Bjurner (eds.) Regional Organizations and Peacemaking; Challengers to the UN Routeledge.

Florini A, Lessons Learned, in Florini ed. (2005) "The Third Force. The Rise of Transnational Civil Society" Carnegie Endowment for International Endowment

Francis D (2009) "Peacekeeping in a Bad Neighborhood; The Economic Community of West African States (ECOWAS) in Peace and Security in West Africa African Journal on Conflict Resolution Vol.1 No 3. Available online http;//dx.doi.org/10.4314/ajcr.v9i3.52180. Accessed 10 August 2016.

Grant R & Keohane R (2005) "Accountability and Abuses in World Politics", Vol. 99 No. 1, February American Political Science Review pp.29-43.

Hamilton G and Wachs B (2008) Putting Economic Governance at the Heart of Peacebuilding United Nations New York and Geneva,

IGAD. 1996. Agreement Establishing the Inter-Government Authority on Development. Assembly of Heads of State and Government. Nairobi; IGAD/SUM-96/AGRE-DOC

IGAD. 2007. IGAD Environment and Natural Resources Strategy. Djibouti, ISBN9966-7255-9-8

IGAD. 2007a. Annual Report of IGAD Executive Secretariat for 2006 and Planned Activities for 2007. Djibouti; IGAD/CM-26/07/WP02

IGAD. 2010a. Communique of the 37th Extra-Ordinary Session of the IGAD Council of Ministers. September 22, New York

Ismail O (2011) "ECOWAS and Human Security" in Thomas Jaye, Dauda Garuba, Stella Amadi (eds) ECOWAS and the Dynamics of Conflict and Peace-Building Council for the Development of Social Science Research in Africa (CODESRIA)

Jeng, A (2012) Peacebuilding in the African Union; Law, Philosophy and Practice (Cambridge University Press)

Kabia J (2011) "Regional Approaches to Peacebuilding; The ECOWAS Peace and Security Architecture". Paper presented at the BISA-Africa and International Studies ESRC seminar series; African Agency in International Politics African Agency in Peace, Conflict and Intervention at the University of Birmingham 7th April.

Killick N, Srikantha, V & Gunduz C (2005) The Role of Local Business in Peacebuilding, Bergh of Research Center for Constructive Conflict Management Available online http;// edoc.vifapol.de/opus/volltexte/2011/2593/ Accessed on 10 August 2016.

Knopf, Kate Almquist. 2016. Ending South Sudan's Civil War. Council on Foreign Relations, Center for Preventive Action, Council Special Report no. 77, November 2016

Kroc Institute for International Peace Studies P (2014) Regional Organizations and Peacebuilding The role of Civil Society, Policy Brief October. Available online. http://www.gppac. net/documents/130492842/0/Regional+Organizations+and+Peacebuilding+The+Role+of+Civil+Society+(2).pdf/33b07303-3984-4930-9cd4-688925b21b6d Accessed on August 10, 2016

Ladsous, H (2014) "UN peacekeeping operations in Africa; Change in 2013 and priorities for 2014", Speech by Hervé Ladsous UN Under-Secretary General for the Department of Peacekeeping Operations", Chatham House 13 January 2014

Lederach, J. P. (1997). Building Peace: Sustainable Reconciliation in Divided Societies. Washington DC: United States Institute of Peace.

Lederach, J. P. (2003). The Little Book of Conflict Transformation. Intercourse, PA: Good Books.

Lederach, J. P., & Appleby, S, (2010) Strategic Peacebuilding: An Overview. In D. Philpott, & G. Powers, Strategies of Peace: Transforming Conflict in a Violent World (pp. 19-44). New York: Oxford University Press.

Mali-After-Action Review of ECOWAS Initiatives and Responses to the Multidimensional Crises in Mali, November 2013 to February 2014, Report Hereafter the Mali-After Action Review Report.

Mehler, A, Melber, H and Walraven, K (eds) (2013) Africa yearbook Vol.9, politics, economy and society south of the sahara in 2012 Leiden; Brill

Mengisteab, Kidane. 2014. The Horn of Africa. Cambridge and Malden; Polity Press

Mine, Y, Stewart, F, Fakuda-Parr and Mkandawire (2013) Preventing violent conflict in Africa; Inequalities, perception and institutions Palgrave Macmillan

Murunga, Godwin R. and Nasong'o, Shadrack M. (eds.). 2007. Kenya; The Struggle for Democracy. Dakar, London, New York; CODESRIA Books and Zed Books

Musah A (2011) "ECOWAS and Regional Responses to Conflicts" in Thomas Jaye, Dauda Garuba, Stella Amadi (eds.) ECOWAS and the Dynamics of Conflict and Peace-Building. Council for the Development of Social Science Research in Africa (CODESTRIA) 2011 pp. 151-164

New Partnership for Africa's Development, NEPAD (2001) The New partnership for Africa's development http://www. dfa.gov.za/events. Nepad.pdf Accessed 10 August 2016.

Olonisakin F (2011) "ECOWAS; From Economic Integration to Peace-building" in Thomas Jaye, Dauda Garuba, Stella Amadi (eds.) ECOWAS and the Dynamics of Conflict and Peace-Building. Council for the Development of Social Science Research in Africa (CODESRIA) pp. 11-26

Olugbemi J. and V. Adetula (2016) "RECs and Peacebuilding in Africa; Analysis of Legal Frameworks and Concerns for International Law". Paper presented at the Policy Dialogue on Regional Economic Communities and Peace Building in Africa, Institute for Peace and Conflict Resolution, IPCR, Abuja 1-2 September, and Abuja, Nigeria

Packer, C and Rukare, D (2002) "The new African Union and its Constitutive Act" The American Journal of International Law 96 (2), pp.365-379.

Rotberg, Robert I (ed.). 2005. Battling Terrorism in the Horn of Africa. Cambridge, Massachusetts, and Washington, D. C.; Wold Peace Foundation and Brookings Institution Press

Rugumamu S (2009) Does the UN Peacebuilding Commission Change the Mode of Peacebuilding in Africa? Dialogue on Globalization Briefing Paper 8 2009 Friedrich Ebert Stiftung (FES) New York'

Ruppel O.(n.d) Regional Economic Communities and Human Rights in East and southern Africa http://www.kas.de/upload/auslandshomepages/namibia/Human_Rights_in_Africa/9_Ruppel.pdf Accessed on August 10, 2016

Saferworld (2011) China's growing role in African peace and security Saferworld Report

Samatar, Abdi Ismail. 2013. "The Production of Somali Conflict and the Role of Internal and External Actors", in Redie Bereketeab (ed.) The Horn of Africa; Intra-State and Inter-State Conflicts and Security. London; Pluto Press.

Sanda, Julie (2016) "Gendering the discourse on conflict and peacebuilding in Africa" Paper presented at the Policy Dialogue on Regional Economic Communities and Peace Building in Africa, Institute for Peace and Conflict Resolution, IPCR, Abuja 1-2 September, and Abuja.

Schirch, L. (2004). The Little Book of Strategic Peacebuilding: A Vision and Framework for Peace with Justice. Intercourse, PA: Good Books.

Schori, P (2015) "ECOWAS and the AU in Cooperation with the Unite Case of Cote d' Ivoire" Peter Wallensteen and Anders Bjurner (eds) Regional Organizations and Peacemaking; Challengers to the UN Routledge

Security Council Report (2011). Special Research Report No. 2; Working Together for Peace and Security in Africa; The Security Council and the AU Peace and Security Council May 10, 2011 http://www.securitycouncilreport.org/special-research-report/ Last viewed September 1, 2016

Security Council Report (2013) Security Council and the UN Peace Building Commission Special Research Report No. 1 18 April 2013 Available online at securitycouncilreport. org. Accessed on August 20, 2016

Sesay, A (2002) "The role of ECOWAS in promoting peace and security in West Africa", DPMN Bulletin, Vol.IX, No.3 June http://www.dpmf.org/role-ecowas-peace-amadu. html (Accessed 30/09/03)

Sesay, A (2016) "ECOWAS and the limits of peace-making West Africa" Paper presented at the Policy Dialogue on Regional Economic Communities and Peace Building in Africa, Institute for Peace and Conflict Resolution, IPCR, Abuja 1-2 September, and Abuja.

SIPRI (2013) SIPRI Yearbook 2013; Armaments, disarmament and international security Oxford University Press.

Striebinger, Kai (2016) Coordination between the African Union and the Regional Economic Communities. International IDEA Stockholm Sweden 2016. Available Online www.idea. int Accessed on 1st September 2016.

Tschirgi, N (2003) Peacebuilding as the link between security and development; Is the window of opportunity closing? New York; International Peace Academy Studies in Security and Development.

United Nations (1992) An Agenda for Peace; Preventive Diplomacy, Peacemaking and Peace-keeping. A/47/277-S/24111, United Nations, New York, 1992.

United Nations (2015) The Challenge of Sustaining Peace. Report of the Advisory Group of Experts for the 2015 Review of the United Nations Peacebuilding Architecture. June 29, 2015 United Nations document A/69/968-S/2015/490

Wallensteen, P (2012) "Regional peacebuilding; a new challenge" New Routes 17 (4), pp. 3-6.

Wallensteen, P et al (2001) Conflict prevention through development cooperation: An inventory of recent findings – With implications for international development cooperation. Uppsala; Department of Peace and Conflict Research, Uppsala University, Report No. 59.

Woodward, Peter. 2013. Crisis in the Horn of Africa; Politics, Piracy and the Threat of Terror. London and New York; I. B. Tauris

Woodward, Peter. 2013a. "The IGAD and Regional Relations in the Horn of Africa" in Redie Bereketeab (ed.) The Horn of Africa; Intra-State and Inter-State Conflicts and Security. London; Pluto Press

Yordanov, R. A. (2016) The Soviet Union and the Horn of Africa During the Cold War; Between Ideology and Pragmatism. Lanham, Boulder, New York, London; Lexington Books

NAI Policy Dialogue

NAI Policy Dialogue is a series of short reports on policy relevant issues concerning Africa today. Aimed at professionals working within aid agencies, ministries of foreign affairs, NGOs and media, these reports aim to inform the public debate and to generate input in the sphere of policymaking. The writers are researchers and scholars engaged in African issues from several disciplinary points of departure. Most have an institutional connection to the Nordic Africa Institute or its research networks. The reports are internally endorsed and reviewed externally. Here is a complete list of the reports published so far in this series:

1. **Havnevik, Kjell; Bryceson, Deborah; Birgegård, Lars-Erik and Matondi, Prosper.** African Agriculture and The World Bank: Development or Impoverishment? (2007)
2. **Cheru, Fantu and Zack-Williams, Alfred.** The quest for sustainable development and peace: the 2007 Sierra Leone elections (2008)
3. **Coulter, Chris; Persson, Mariam and Utas, Mats.** Young female fighters in African wars: conflict and its consequences (2008)
4. **Utas, Mats.** Sexual abuse survivors and the complex of traditional healing: (G)local Prospects in the Aftermath of an African War (2009)
5. **Eriksson Baaz, Maria and Stern, Maria.** La complexité de la violence: Analyse critique des violences sexuelles en République Démocratique du Congo (2011)
6. **Vogiazides, Louisa.** 'Legal Empowerment of the Poor' versus 'Right to the City': Implications for access to housing in urban Africa (2012)
7. **Vainio, Antti.** Market-based and Rights-based Approaches to the Informal Economy: A comparative analysis of the policy implications (2012)
8. **Gelot, Linnéa; Gelot, Ludwig and de Coning, Cedric.** Supporting African peace operations (2012)
9. **Eriksson Baaz, Maria and Utas, Mats.** Beyond "Gender and Stir": Reflections on gender and SSR in the aftermath of African conflicts (2012)
10. **Follér, Maj-Lis; Haug, Christoph; Knutsson, Beniamin and Thörn, Håkan.** Who is responsible?: Donor-civil society partnerships and the case of hiv/aids work (2013)
11. **Nlandu Mayamba Mbuya, Thierry.** Building a Police Force "for the good" in DR Congo: Questions that still haunt reformers and reform beneficiaries (2013)
12. **Adetula, Victor A.O; Bereketeab, Redie and Jaiyebo, Olugbemi.** Regional Economic Communities and Peacebuilding in Africa: The Experiences of ECOWAS and IGAD (2016)

www.ingramcontent.com/pod-product-compliance
Lightning Source LLC
Chambersburg PA
CBHW060843270326
41933CB00003B/181